Messerschmitt
Bf 110 ZERSTÖRER
in action

by JERRY L. CAMPBELL

illustrated by Don Greer

 squadron/signal publications

[Cover] Lt. Hans-Joachim Jabs of II/ZG 76 gets his fifth and sixth victory over Dunkirk.

For my daughters:
Lori & Jill Campbell

ISBN 0-89747-029-X

If you have any photographs of the aircraft, armor, soldiers or ships of any nation, particularly wartime snapshots, why not share them with us and help make Squadron/Signal's books all the more interesting and complete in the future. Any photograph sent to us will be copied and the original returned. The donor will be fully credited for any photos used. Please send them to: Squadron/Signal Publications, Inc.. 1115 Crowley Dr., Carrollton, TX 75011-5010.

Photo Credits

Bundesarchiv
Hans Seebrandf
Smithsonian
Gustav Tham
Wolfgang Falck
Bob Grinsell
Werner Held
U.S. Air Force
Hans-Joachim Jabs
Gene Stafford
Ossie Anttonen
Russian News Service
Ernie McDowell
Hans Redemann
Mihai Moisescu
Lee Barlow

Bf 110 Zerstörer

The strategic fighter concept was first evolved during the air battles of WWI when the air forces of both sides found themselves in need of a fighter that could penetrate deep into enemy territory escorting bombers, attacking hostile aircraft and targets far behind enemy lines. Technology did not permit such an aircraft to evolve during the 1914-1918 war and during the twenties lack of interest in military aviation delayed the resurrection of the concept until the middle thirties when the rise of Nazi Germany gave new impetus to the development of military hardware both inside and outside of Germany.

1934 can be pointed to as the year of the strategic fighter. In Poland the P.Z.L. P.38 Wolf won a design competition, in France specifications for a strategic fighter were issued, and in Germany specifications for a Kampfzerstörer design were given out.

The concept of a strategic fighter, or Kampfzerstörer (Battle-destroyer), as it became known in Germany, caught the imagination of Hermann Göring who was ultimately responsible for issuing the specifications for a multipurpose strategic fighter capable of:

1. penetrating deep into enemy territory in order to clear the skies of enemy opposition ahead of bomber formations;
2. escorting and providing close defense for bomber formations;
3. the interception and destruction of offensive enemy bomber formations;
4. carrying out bombing and strike as well as ground attack missions.

The technical design specifications calling for a twin engine all metal three seat monoplane armed with heavy cannon and an internal bombbay, were presented to AGO (Arado), Dornier, Focke-Wulf, Heinkel, Henschel, Gotha and BFW (Bayerische Flugzeugwerke - Messerschmitt).

BFW, Focke-Wulf and Henschel all submitted design proposals. Focke-Wulf and Henschel, both of which had submitted design proposals very close to the original specifications, were immediately awarded a contract for three prototypes each, Focke-Wulf for the Fw 57 and Henschel for the Hs 124. BFW, however, had ignored many of the Kampfzerstörer specifications, concentrating instead on performance and it was only through pressure brought to bear by Ernst Udet that BFW was finally awarded a prototype contract under the designation Bf 110.

The Focke-Wulf entry, the Fw 57, was the largest of the Kampfzerstörer designs with a wing span of 82 ft. and was powered by a pair of 910 h.p. DB 600 12 cylinder liquid cooled engines. Armament featured two forward firing 20mm MG FF cannon projecting through a glazed nose and a single MG FF cannon in an electrically-operated Mauser dorsal turret. The Henschel Hs 124 was powered by a pair of Junkers Jumo 21OC 12 cylinder liquid-cooled inverted V engines of 600 h.p. Forward firing cannon armament was to be mounted in a Mauser turret and an internal bomb bay was provided. Before prototype fabrication could begin, however, the RLM had second thoughts concerning the bomber requirement of the design and requested a purely Zerstörer aircraft and issued separate specifications for a Schnellbomber. The Messerschmitt design team which had in fact almost completely ignored the bomber portion of the technical requirements and in so doing produced the purely Zerstörer aircraft that the requirements now called for.

The Bf 110 had the long sleek lines of a fighter and was powered by a pair

The Bf 110V 1 was taken aloft for the first time on 12 May 1936 with Rudolf Opitz at the controls. The machine was extremely underpowered and flight testing suffered constant interruption due to frequent breakdowns of the DB 600A engines.

The preproduction Bf 110A-0s were powered by a pair of 680 h.p. Junker Jumo 210Da engines turning VDM-Hamilton two bladed variable pitch propellers.

of Daimler Benz DB 600A engines, wing leading edges featured Handley Page automatic slots and the tail had a twin fin rudder arrangement. The first prototype, the Bf 11OV1, was taken aloft for the first time by Rudolf Opitz on 12 May 1936 at Augsburg and a few days later a speed of 314 mph was attained in level flight. Unfortunately the DB 600A engines were proving to be extremely unreliable and the aircraft was found to swing violently during take-off and landing, providing the very real possibility of ground looping. Adjusting the undercarriage camber alleviated the swing on landing and take-off (the problem was never completely solved).

The powerplant problem was not so easily solved and because of this it was not until 24 October 1936 that the second prototype, the Bf 11OV2, was finished. Assigned directly to the Luftwaffe test center at Rechlin, the test pilots were pleased with its speed but somewhat dissatisfied with its maneuverability. It's speed, however, was faster than the Bf 109B-1 then being supplied to the Jagdflieger and consequently an initial order for four preproduction A-Os were ordered. In January 1937 the Bf 11OV2 was

delivered to the Rechlin test center for evaluation by Air Ministry test pilots. The Hs 124 and Fw 57, because they had more closely followed the original specifications, were declared unsuitable for the purely Zerstörer role. The Bf 110 Zerstörer was now ordered into full production with all possible speed.

Willi Messerschmitt's design had not however won solely by default. The twin engine machine not only met the 'new' requirements but in some areas exceeded them. The four Bf 11OA-O preproduction machines for service evaluation were to be powered by a pair 986 h.p. DB 600Aa engines. By the time preproduction A-Os were ready for engines, however, the DB 600Aa was declared unsuitable for fighter installation and a pair 610 h.p. Junkers Jumo 210B engines were installed instead. The first preproduction machine was finished during August 1937 and proved to be considerably under-powered, attaining a top speed of only 268 mph. The A-O differed from the Versuch (test) series in being armed with four forward firing 7.9mm MG 17 machine guns mounted in the nose; the tails of the engine nacelles were reduced in depth and increased in length; the tail wheel was made non-retractable and a rearward firing flexible 7.9mm MG 15 was added at the rear of the green house.

In anticipation of the newer and more powerful DB 601 engine, an assembly line was set up to begin turning out production machines during early spring of 1938. Further delays in certifying the power plant however were encountered preventing production schedules from being met.

It has been often times suggested that the Luftwaffe was extremely unhappy at the performance of the BF 110 at the time of its introduction. Nothing could be further from the truth. The Bf 110 was as fast as any single engine fighter found in the arsenal of Germany's enemies. If it was somewhat sluggish on the controls, its heavy fire power and the evolution of new tactics were expected to be able to overcome this problem. In short, the Luftwaffe was delighted with its new weapon. It was a war machine that an elite force could be built around: The Zerstörergruppen.

Shortly after the RLM changed the Kampfzerstörer design the Luftwaffe issued specifications to evolve the Bf 110 to the Fernaufklärer [reconnaissance] and Schnellbomber [fast bomber] roles under the designation Bf 161 and Bf 162 respectively. It was decided to drop the Aufklärer in favor of adopting the standard Bf 110 to the reconnaissance role and the Bf 162 fast bomber lost out to the Ju 88. [Hans Seebrandt]

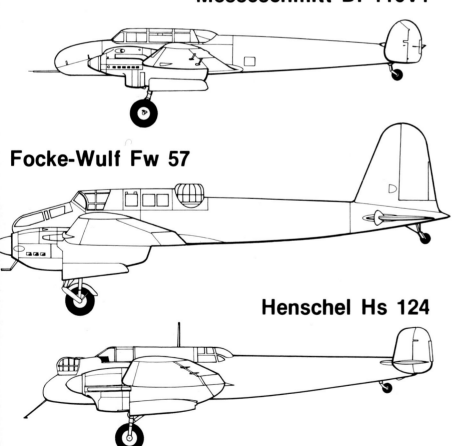

Messeschmitt Bf 110V1

Focke-Wulf Fw 57

Henschel Hs 124

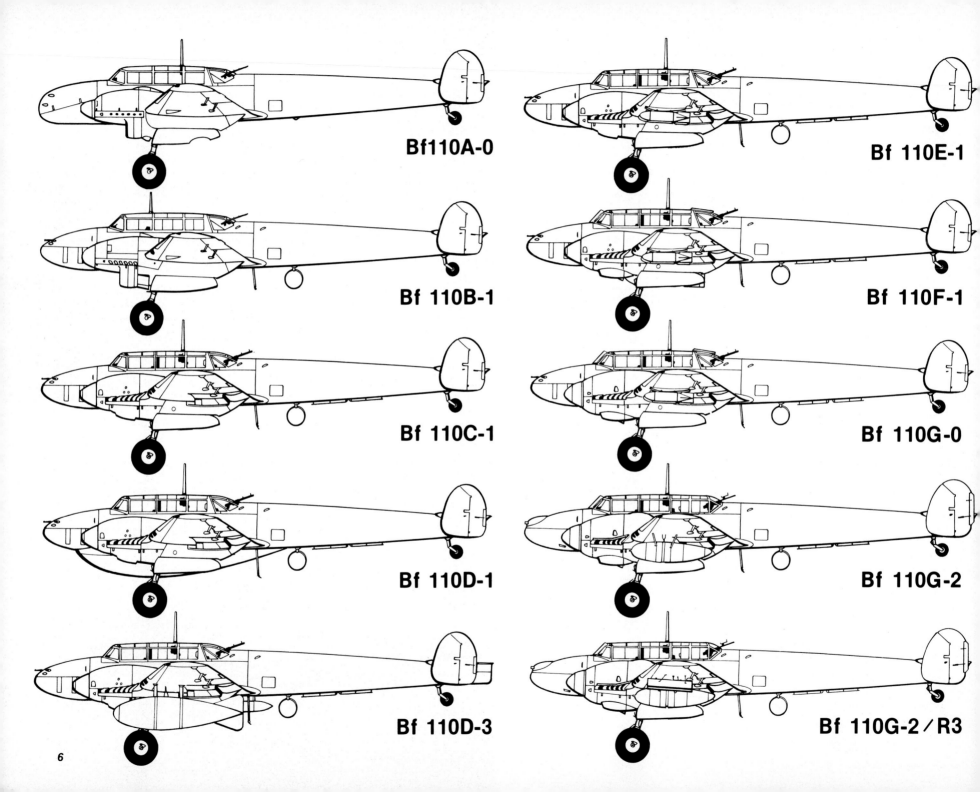

Bf110A-0

Bf 110B-1

Bf 110C-1

Bf 110D-1

Bf 110D-3

Bf 110E-1

Bf 110F-1

Bf 110G-0

Bf 110G-2

Bf 110G-2／R3

Bf 110B

By March 1938 BFW had begun series production of a refined version of the Zerstörer. The nose section had been redesigned into more aerodynamically pleasing lines and a pair of 20mm MG FF cannon were added firing through openings in the lower portion of the new nose.

Unfortunately, by the time the airframes had reached an advanced stage in construction the DB 601A engines had still not been certified for installation so it was decided that an up-powered version of the Jumo engine would continued to be used. In April the first preproduction Bf 110B-O took to the air powered by a pair of Jumo 210Ga engines of 700 h.p. each. In July 1938 the first production Bf 110B-1s began to roll off the assembly line. The Luftwaffe took the visit of the French Chief of Air Staff, General Vuillemin, during August, as an opportunity to unveil their new twin engine aircraft. The General was conducted to Augsburg where he was allowed to witness a fire-power demonstration and the production lines of the Zerstörer. Bf 110B-1s were seen to role off the assembly line at regular intervals and fly away. What the French Chief of Air Staff did not know was that the preproduction Bf 110B-Os and the few Bf-110B-1s were being rolled out and flown away only to land out of sight and be rolled off the assembly line again.

Only some 45 machines were produced, before production of the Jumo powered aircraft was terminated. I(Zerstörer)/LG1, a training Gruppe, was issued some of them, as were I/ZG 1(formerly JG141) and I/ZG 76 (formerly III/JG 132) which placed them in a training staffel.

Development of the B series was as follows:

Bf 110B-1 Zerstörer, carried the full forward firing armament, four 7.92mm machine guns, a pair of 20mm MG FF cannons.

Bf 110B-2 Reconnaissance version with the cannon removed and a camera installed.

Bf 110B-3 Trainer with the cannon removed and additional radio equipment installed. A number of B-1s were modified to this standard.

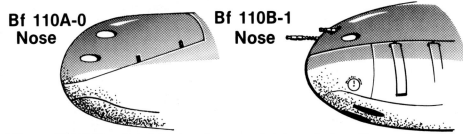

Bf 110A-0 Nose

Bf 110B-1 Nose

[Above Right] The B-1 introduced a completely redesigned nose through which two of the four 7.9 mm MG 17 machine guns now protruded. The lower portion of the nose now mounted a pair of 20 mm MG FF cannon whose blast tube opening can just be seen at the bottom of the nose. [Smithsonian Institution]

[Right] The gaping radiators are the most identifiable feature of the Bf 110B. The B series remained standard with the Zerstörerschulen until well into 1941. [Hans Seebrandt]

During the winter of 1938-39 Bf 110B-1s were issued to I/ZG 1 and I/ZG 76, forming a Zerstörerschulstaffel in each Gruppe. The training and development Geschwader LG 1 also received the B-1 forming I[Z]/LG 1. The above machines belong to I/ZG 76 [Gustav Tham]

[Above Right] Not only did the Zerstörerschulen train aircrew but they also trained ground crew. These Schwarzmenschen [Black Men], named for their black coveralls, are seen changing a burst tire at Nancy during 1941. [Hans Seebrandt]

Most of the surviving Bf 110B aircraft were eventually passed to Zerstörerschulen where they were modified to the B-3 standard — cannon armament removed and additional radio equipment installed. [Hans Seebrandt]

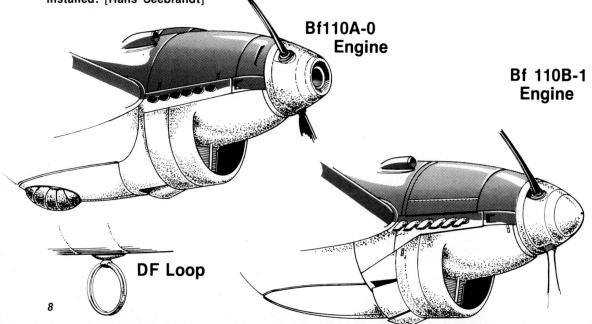

Bf110A-0 Engine

Bf 110B-1 Engine

DF Loop

Bf 110C

In late 1938 the DB 601A-1 was finally certified for installation in production aircraft. The intervening months had not been lost, the design team had spent the time well, refining and perfecting the new aircraft. The deep bath radiators under each engine were removed and replaced by a shallow glycol radiator beneath the wing trailing edge just outboard of each engine. Small oil coolers were introduced into the lower portion of the engine nacelle and the wing tips were squared off, cutting down the overall wing span by just over two feet. The port engine carburator intake was moved to an opening in the wing just outboard of the engine nacelle. Maximum speed was 336 mph at 20,000 feet, normal range was 680 miles, and with auxilliary fuel tanks this was increased to 876 miles.

By the end of January 1939 production Bf 110C-1 machines were being delivered to I(Z)/LG 1, a training and development Gruppe at Greifswald. Production tempo continued to increase so that during spring and early summer I/ZG 1 and I/ZG 76 received their aircraft.

France, the first foreign country to view the Bf 110 when General Vuillemin visited Augsburg in August 1938, in May 1939, became the first foreign country to possess a Bf 110. A mechanic and his brother, a pilot working in the Augsburg plant, were paid by the French Secret Service to steal a Zerstörer and fly it to France. Unfortunately for the brothers weather conditions were such that they were both killed during a crash landing in France. After two months of examination, the aircraft was returned to Germany.

Bf 110C-1 Zerstörer

Bf 110C-2 Zerstörer - differing in having a FuG 10 instead of the earlier FuG III a U radio.

Bf 110C-3 Zerstörer - an improved MG-FF cannon.

Bf 110C-4 Zerstörer - armour protection added for the crew.

Bf 110C-4/B Jabo A fighter-bomber fitted with a pair of ETC 250 bomb racks under the fuselage just behind the leading edge of the wing allowing a pair of 551 lb. bombs to be carried. Power was provided by a pair of DB 601N engines in place of the DB 601A-1.

Bf 110C-5 Reconnaissance variant with the MG-FF cannon removed and an Rb 50/30 camera mounted on the cockpit floor.

Bf 110C-5/N Reconnaissance variant similar to the C-5 above except for the addition of DB 601N engine.

Bf 110C-6 Zerstörer - the two 20mm MG-FF cannons were replaced by a single 30mm Rheinmetall MK 101 cannon.

Bf 110C-7 Jabo carried an ETC 500 rack on the fuselage centerline increasing bomb load to a pair of 1,102 lb. bombs. Power was provided by a pair of DB 601N engines.

The deep bath radiators under the engines were replaced by shallow glycol radiators mounted under the wings forward of the flaps. This not only solved an excessive turbulance problem but also made maintenance somewhat easier. [Bundesarchiv]

The initial production Bf 110C-1s were delivered to I[Z]/LG 1 at Greifswald during January, 1939. The C-1 series standardized on the new UDM three-bladed, controllable, full-feathering prop. [Bundesarchiv]

Shallow Wing Glycol Radiator

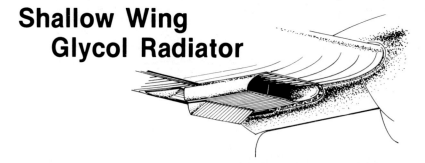

The period immediately prior to the invasion of Poland was spent converting single engine fighter Gruppen to the new twin engine machines and training the air crew to fly them. This novice Zerstörer pilot [left] double checks his map coordinate with his gunner before a cross-country training flight.

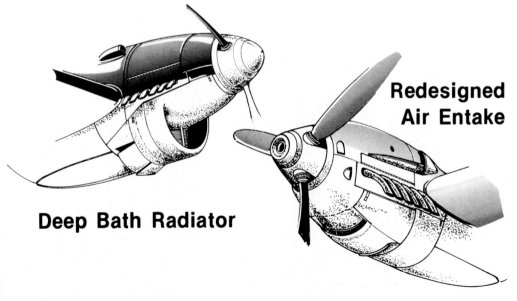

Deep Bath Radiator

Redesigned Air Entake

A special hydraulic jack was provided that fit under the landing gear oleo lifting the aircraft free of the ground allowing the "black ones" to easily replace a worn or damaged tire. [Bundesarchiv]

The Bf 110 in Combat: Poland

On 1 September Operation White, the Invasion of Poland, began and Göring's elite Zerstörer units were in the thick of fighting from the beginning; I(Z)/LG 1 and I/ZG 1 were assigned to Luftflotte 1 (Kesselring) along the Polish-East Prussian border and I/ZG 76 was in the south with Luftflotte 4 (Lohr) along the Polish-Czechoslavakian border.

It may be that 2./ZG 76 had the honor of being the first Zerstörer unit to cross the Polish frontier. Wolfgang Falck, a young Oberleutnant and Staffelkapitän of 2./ZG 76 at the time, relates: "We had been briefed to takeoff at 06.00 and escort He 111s of KG 4 to Krakow. In our enthusiasm someone suggested that maybe we should take off early in order to steal an hour of combat on the other Zerstörer." A suggestion was all it took as each pilot raced for his machine in order not to be left behind. "Unfortunately we did not find our bombers until we got over Krakow, happily there was nothing to protect them from, not even flak, just a few little white clouds. After the bombers unloaded we escorted them back to the frontier. As I neared the frontier I could see villages burning and I finally felt that a war had begun. Since our fuel was getting low we turned toward our airfield leaving the bombers behind. As we banked away from the Heinkels I looked down and there was a Heinkel 46 army reconnaissance aircraft looking very lonely down there with no protection. I dove down to escort him saying aloud to myself, 'look, we are here, you can do your job under our wings!' All of a sudden he saw me and started to twist and turn like crazy and the gunner blazed away at me. Pulling away I realized I had just gotten my baptism of fire from one of our own aircraft. A few minutes later I saw another aircraft flying. 'Ha! a PZL 23, I can start my score.' As I tried to gain some height he curved into the sun and as he did I caught a glimpse of red on his wing - I'm sure he's a Polish aircraft now. We had been briefed that the normal red and white box insignia had the white overpainted with camouflage leaving only the red visible. As I turned into him I opened fire, but fortunately, my marksmanship was no better than the reconnaissance gunner's had been, as he banked to get away I saw it was a Stuka. I then realized that what I had thought was a red Polish insignia was actually a red E. I reported this immediately after landing and before long the colored letters on wings of our aircraft were overpainted in black." Falck and I/ZG 76 remained scoreless on the first day.

In the Northern Sector, the Bf 110 equipped I(Z)/LG 1 escorted He 111Ps of KG 27 against Warsaw. As the Heinkels prepared to drop their bombs, thirty PZL 11Cs of the Pawlikowski's Pursuit Brigade rose to give battle, within minutes the Zerstörer had blown five of the nimble Polish fighters out of the air without a loss to themselves. The Bf 110 had drawn its first blood.

On the second day I/ZG 76 met a number of PZL 11s over Lodz with Leutnant Helmuth Lent and Oberleutnant Nagel shooting down one each. The Polish pilots, however, were able to shoot down three of the Zerstörer.

Organized activity on the part of the Polish Air Force diminished very quickly with most of their number being destroyed on the ground and the Zerstörer began to carry out ground attack and strike missions. Occasional enemy air activity was encountered. Oberleutnant Wolfgang Falck, credited with three kills during the Polish Campaign, described his first kill:

This Bf 110C-1 of 2./ZG 76 stands among the trees in Czechoslovakia after having been fueled and armed on the evening of 31 August. The red "D" is outlined white.

I[Z]/LG 1 carried a wolf's head on the nose of it's Bf 110Cs. This Zerstörer training unit was part of Luftflotte 1 [Kesselring] taking part in Operation White from East Prussia, and in fact scored the first Zerstörer blood when five PZL 11s were shot down without loss. [Bundesarchiv]

We were flying 'Freijagd' (free hunting) deep in Polish territory when I saw an aircraft similar to a Ju 87. When I got closer I could see that it was a PZL 23. It was no contest, I guess he was flying along enjoying the morning sun.

On the 10th of September Staffelkapitän Falck was ordered to report to Göring at Breslau (Wroclaw) in southerwestern Poland.

When we arrived we were briefed that we would have the honor of escorting Field Marshal Göring's Ju 52 over the battle area. After the flight briefing I was invited to the Field Marshal's personal train car to have coffee with him and his staff and was asked about my experiences of the past 10 days. At the end of my report, Göring made a signal to one of his staff who handed me a paper bag with an Iron Cross in it. While the paper bag took some of the drama out of the occasion, receiving one of the first Iron Crosses of the war certainly swelled my chest with pride.

Air activity over Poland now was solely a Luftwaffe affair and on 17 September the Red Army crossed the Polish Frontier in five places and by 28 September Poland was completely subjugated and divided between Russia and Germany. The Zerstörer had acquitted itself extremely well in combat and a smug Göring pointed to his elite Zerstörer with a great deal of pride. Bf 110 losses to all causes were only twelve machines.

[Right] 2./ZG 76 on their first mission over Poland took off an hour early in order to steal combat experience on the other Zerstörer units. Staffelkapitän Falck's "G" flies the lead position. [Wolfgang Falck]

[Bottom Center] The pilots of I[Z]/LG 1 were the first Zerstörers to draw blood when they were met over Warsaw by the Pawlikowski's Pursuit Brigade. Note the unusual practice of painting a kill marking on the nose instead of the tail. [Bundesarchiv]

[Bottom Right] Oblt. Falck showing his Iron Cross to his ground crew after his return from Breslau. [Wolfgang Falck]

The unit insignia of 2./ZG 76 was red bodied lady bug with seven black dots on its back and a black head on a white shield. Oberleutnant Falck is at the controls and Feldwebel Alfred Walz is bordfunker. [Wolfgang Falck]

Battle of Heligoland Bight

After the Polish Campaign, I/ZG 76 transferred to the Rhine area flying patrols along the Franco-German border, on 17 December this crack Zerstörer unit was posted to Jever to reinforce "Kommando Schumacher" in the face of increased RAF activity in the Heligoland Bight area. The next day twenty-two Wellingtons of No. 9, 37 and 149 Squadrons carried out an "armed reconnaissance". The RAF force was picked up by Freya radar while still far out to sea. "Kommando Schumacher" put thirty-two Bf 109s and sixteen Bf 110s in the air. Only 10 Wellingtons returned to England and of the 12 lost, nine were claimed by the Bf 110s of I/ZG 76.

Staffelkapitän Falck and his wing man were on patrol north west of Borkum not far from the island of Taxel. "We flew in the direction of Heligoland and when we sighted the enemy we began climbing. The bombers were quite a distance away and we could see small puffs of smoke as flak burst over Wilhelmshaven as the tommies turned toward England". Diving to the attack Falck got one Wellington and his wing man, Feldwebel Fresia, got two before they had to break off their attack when Falck's machine took hits from the tail turret of a Wellington. "With both engines stopped, I glided to the airfield on Wangerooge Island - it was the first and last time that I was a glider pilot".

Bf 110C-F Canopy

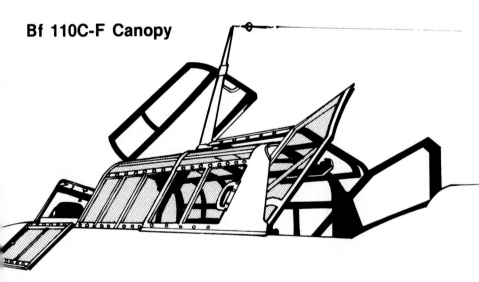

[Above Right] Flying in a tight defensive formation, the Wellingtons of 149 Squadron finding no targets at sea bank into a turn over Wilhelmshaven. Disaster is only minutes away.

Falck and the proud pilots of 2./ZG 76 line up in front of the young Staffelkapitän's machine at Jever airfield shortly after the Battle of Heligoland Bight. Nine of twelve Wellingtons lost were shot down by ZG 76. [Wolfgang Falck]

During early spring JG 144 traded their Bf 109s for Bf 110s and was renamed II/ZG 76. Adopting the sharkmouth as their emblem they became known as the Haifisch Gruppe [shark group]. Seen here shortly after the new Zerstörergruppe received their new machines is Hans-Joachim Jabs who would become one of the top night fighter aces and Kommodore of NJG 1. [Hans-Joachim Jabs via Bob Grinsell]

After training with the Erganzungs [Zerstörer] staffel, Lt. Gustav Tham joined II/ZG 76. ZG 76, one of the first Zerstörer units that began painting the nose cover in the staffel color, was stationed along the relatively quiet Franco-German border during the Scandinavian operations. [Gustav Tham]

OPERATION WESERÜBUNG

The Bf 110 had now proven itself in battle and by the beginning of 1940 production had surpassed 100 per month. I and II/ZG 26 had converted from BF 109s, and in February I/JG 144 traded in their Bf 109s becoming II/ZG 76, bringing the total number of Zerstörergruppen to five operational gruppen; I and II/ZG 2 and III/ZG 26 and I/ZG 52 were also being organized. Göring's plans were to fill the skies with his elite Zerstörer.

On 8 April Oberleutnant Falck, having been promoted to Gruppen Kommandeur of I/ZG 1, was ordered to the Hotel Esplanade, 10. Fliegerdivision Headquarters in Hamburg. When he arrived he was taken to a locked room already full of Gruppen Kommandeurs and was told that Germany would occupy Denmark and Norway the next morning.

Denmark

Each of us received our individual orders and were informed that after we had left, most of our ground crewmen had been loaded into trucks and would cross into Denmark the next morning along with the second wave of infantry; those gruppen going to Norway would have their ground crews flown in with the airborne infantry units right after paratroopers secured the airfields. I was ordered to take two staffeln to Denmark where we were to patrol in the area of Copenhagen and then land at Aalborg, our other staffel was sent to Norway. The briefing officer told us that we could expect the Danish people to be 'very surprised and very happy to have the German forces liberate them, but if any planes try to take off we should let none escape'. That night my aircrews and I sat around discussing the coming 'Liberation' and I decided that we would fly as low as possible across the Baltic and then climb to 500 meters with the rising sun at our backs after we cross the coastline. If the Danes are happy to receive us, fine, but if we are to meet an enemy over Copenhagen I want my boys to have any edge I can give them. The next morning the weather is fine and we take off from Barth at daybreak. We fly low, low, low, not more than 5 to 10 meters above the water. It was such a short flight we didn't have to use maps - the beach loomed ahead, we crossed a road, then a rail line and as we pulled up I could see our target, the main airfield on the outskirts of Copenhagen. On the tarmac below were 10 old high wing Fokker reconnaissance aircraft and about two dozen Fokker D-21 fighters lined up in the morning sun, and they all seemed to be warming up. If they got into the air we would have our hands full - dog-fighting with a D-21 at low altitude would be no mean task. Just then I spotted one of the recce's taking off. As I went for the Fokker, now about 100 meters in the air, the others began strafing the now taxiing fighters as ground fire opened up on us. Firing both my cannon and MG's, the recce' burst into flames and fell back to the ground as I pulled up. I banked around and saw fire and smoke billowing up from the burning aircraft on the ground. So much for the 'happy welcome to our liberation'.

I was making my third pass against the airfield when my machine shuddered and my left engine stopped. A second later I got a kick in the best part of my anatomy so hard that it threw me against the top of my greenhouse - I was hit. I had heard that the first minutes after being hit you felt no pain, only numbness. I felt the needle pricks of numbness in my buttocks and thighs. I don't think I can make the long flight over enemy territory to Aalborg, so I turn over command to one of my staffelkapitäns and decide to fly south so I can at least crash land behind German lines. I fly along the main road on one engine, hoping to see German tanks. I know I must be hit bad, since I still can't feel anything and I'm probably losing a lot of blood. I raise up trying to feel for the wound, but with my flying suit and parachute in the way I can't find anything wet. I decide I'll be the hero, so I strike out across the sea toward Barth. I can fly from ship to ship in case I have to ditch in the water. I'm feeling weak from the loss of blood, but I'm responsible for my back seater, so I keep pushing myself on, getting weaker and weaker. At last I see Barth ahead and come in to land on one engine. As we roll to a stop, I unbuckle and open the greenhouse hood. Shakily I stand up, I can't see any blood on the seat and my gunner says he can't see any blood on my flying suit. I climb out on the wing and lower myself to the ground. Looking under the aircraft, I find a hole that shouldn't be there just under the cockpit. I climb back on the wing and look into the cockpit. The leather gasket around the control stick was torn away - a bullet had come into the cockpit. I take off my parachute and open it up. There are 54 folds in a parachute, and there, in the last fold, is the bullet that knocked me against the roof of the cockpit. Without acknowledging the grins on the faces surrounding me, I commandeer another machine and head back into the battle. Using the same flight pattern, I again pop up from the ground and come out of the sun over the Danish airfield. The ground is littered with smoking skeletons of burned out aircraft. The soldiers run like mad when they see me, but there is no fire from the ground, even so, I decide not to land and be 'welcomed'. Turning toward the northwest, I head for Aalborg where my unit should be waiting. On the way, I see one of my Bf 110's that has force-landed in a meadow. Banking around, I can see the pilot standing on the wing surrounded by a mob of Danish soldiers. "A bad situation! What do I do?" I decided to take a chance and land, as I taxi over to the downed aircraft, there is no overt hostility from the Danish troops. The pilot explains that he was hit by ground fire and had been treated very well by the Danes who were under the command of a young captain to whom he introduces me. The pilot has already been in touch with Aalborg, which was in our hands after a paratroop drop of only a platoon. Aalborg was already sending a replacement engine. I thanked the Danish captain for the treatment of my pilot, got back in my aircraft and continued on to Aalborg.

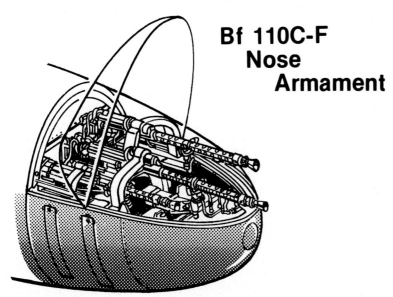

Bf 110C-F Nose Armament

The pilot of a Bf 110 wore a seat-pack parachute similiar to the parachute worn by pilots of single engine fighters and the radio operator-gunner wore the standard back-pack parachute. The position of the seat-pack parachute undoubtedly saved the life of Wolfgang Falck when it stopped a machine gun bullet, when his unarmored C-1 was hit by ground fire. [Werner Held]

Norway

In Norway the situation proved to be quite different from the quick and relatively easy occupation of Denmark. Seaborne landings were carried out at five separate points along the Norwegian coast. At zero hour plus 175 minutes, Bf 110s of I/ZG 76 were to arrive over Oslo-Fornebu and Stavanger-Sola airfields to clear the skies of enemy aircrat, and provide top cover and ground support for the Fallschirmjäger (paratroopers) who were to arrive some ten minutes later. Twenty minutes later, after the paratroopers had landed and hopefully had the field secure, Ju 52s would arrive, land and disgorge assault infantry to begin securing the surrounding area and prevent a counter attack. A simple plan, but one that allowed for little deviation in the time table - the Bf 110s would have only twenty minutes of fuel left when they arrived over the target.

Oberleutnant Hansen, leading eight Bf 110s of 1./ZG 76, was on time over Fornebu when nine Gloster Gladiators attacked out of the sun. In the wild dog fight that ensued two Zerstörer and three Gladiators were lost before the Norwegian Biplanes were driven off. The fight had left three of Hansen's six remaining aircraft flying on only one engine and used up any extra fuel they might have had. Circling the Norwegian airfield Hansen saw no sign of the paratroopers, unknown to Hansen the 29 Ju 52s of II/KGzb VI carrying the Fallschirmjäger had in fact encountered extremely bad weather and turned back! At 0845 Hansen ordered his three remaining intact machines to begin strafing the ground defenses, softening them up, getting ready for the arrival of paratroopers that were not coming. At 0905 as their last drops of fuel were being used Hansen saw Ju 52s appear through clouds in the distance. Assuming this was the late arrival of the paratroopers when, in fact, it was the early arrival of the assault infantry, 1./ZG 76 began getting into position to concentrate their fire on the machine gun emplacements that could be murderous to the paratroopers while they hung in the air.

The infantry laden 'Iron Annies', not knowing that the paratroopers had never shown up, went immediately into a landing pattern. Oblt. Hansen watched in amazement as the lead ship, instead of disgorging paratroopers, swept in to land, lurched under heavy ground fire and began to pull up. Hansen, realizing he could wait no longer decided that if the paratroopers couldn't take the airfield, ZG 76 would. 'Lent, go in and land! We'll give you covering fire.' With only one engine turning and black smoke pouring out of the other, Lent streaked down the runway with machine gun bullets splashing around him. Narrowly missing a Ju 52 trying to land on a second runway, Lent's machine crashed through the perimeter fence snapping off both landing gears and slid to rest in front of a wooden house on the edge of the airfield. One after the other the remaining five Bf 110s of 1./ZG 76 touched down on the runway and taxied to the northwest perimeter of the airfield where they lined up with their rear machine guns trained on the Norwegian positions. Within minutes Lent and his radio operator, Kubisch, showed up carrying the flexible MG 15 and some ammo drums. Fortunately there was no fire fight - the Norwegian troops had begun withdrawing even as Lent had touched down. The 1. Staffel of Zerstörer Geschwader 76 had captured the airfield. At 0917 the Ju 52s of II/KGzbV 1 began landing, flooding the field with assault troops, also in this wave were the mechanics of ZG 76 who immediately begin the task of repairing the damaged Zerstörer.

An Unteroffizier of ZG 76s ground crew uses chalk to put a temporary victory mark on the tail of Falck's machine after the occupation of Denmark. [Wolfgang Falck]

The machines of 1./ZG 76 lined up along the Northwest perimeter with their rear machine guns trained on the Norwegian positions. [Bundesarchiv]

Meanwhile on the southwest coast at Stavanger-Sola airfield quite the reverse had been going on. The Fallschirmjäger of 3./FJR 1 had dropped nearly on time after being slowed up by weather conditions but their air support, the Bf 110s of 3./ZG 76 under Oblt. Gollob, had encountered such adverse weather that all but two aircraft had been forced to turn back. In the face of heavy ground fire and without air cover the paratroopers had jumped onto Sola airfield. As the paratroopers began trying to collect themselves under withering defensive fire the two Zerstörer of 3./ZG 76 screamed across the airfield with their guns and cannon blazing, scattering the Norwegian defenders, giving the Fallschirmjäger time to organize their attack. After a half-hour of heavy fighting the airfield was in German hands and the Bf 110s could land, with the Ju 52s carrying reinforcements right behind them.

Berlin had hoped that Norway would lay down its arms as the Danes had done, but this was not to be the case, heavy fighting continued and on the 13th a hastily put together British Expeditionary Force landed. Heavy ground fighting continued for over a month but most of the German air units including the Zerstörer were quickly withdrawn and deployed along the Franco-German border. The Scandinavian campaign cost the Luftwaffe just over twenty Bf 110s.

Lt. Helmut Lent's Bf 110 after shearing off the landing gear came to rest in the front yard of a house on the edge of Oslo-Fornebu airfield.

German fighter units, as did their Allied counterparts, kept a score board listing their victories. This board, belonging to I/ZG 76, shows their victories through 12 April. [Hans Seebrandt]

Bf110C-2, C-3 and C-4

Operations and technology dictated changes and improvements in the Bf 110s in order to make the Zerstörer more effective and versatile in combat. The C-2, already in service during the Norwegian campaign, differed from the C-1 only by having the improved FuG 10. Before the invasion of France began the Bf 110C-3 with an improved MG FF—lacking the external breech fairing—began rolling off the assembly line. Very quickly the C-3 gave way to C-4 which for the first time provided armor plated protection for the crew. Going into production at the beginning of the offensive in the West, the C-4 did not arrive at the front in substantial numbers until the Battle of Britain began.

Offensive in the West

The German war plan for the subjugation of the West called for a breakthrough in the Ardennes between Namur and Montmedy and then a wide armored sweep towards the Channel coast at the mouth of the Somme. If this was to be carried out the northern flank, Holland and Belgium, had to be secured from British and French use. As in previous operations the Zerstörergruppen were called upon to clear the air of enemy fighters and to carry out air strikes deep behind enemy lines as well as to escort bomber formations.

At dawn on 10 May 1940 the 'Sitzkrieg' was over as the German armed forces launched their massive assault against France and the Low Countries. ZG 1 and ZG 26 were assigned to Luftflotte 2 (Kesselring) operating in support of Army Group B's invasion of Holland and Belgium and ZG 76 was assigned to Luftflotte 3 (Sperrle) operating in support of the Army Group A whose task was to strike through Luxembourg and southern Belgium into France. I/ZG 1 was transferred to Kirchheim in anticipation of the attack on the low countries. As Falck explains it:

One day Kesselring came to visit, we were sitting and talking about the possibility of an attack against the West when he gave me our orders. Our Gruppe was to attack and destroy aircraft on airfields in Holland. I led a staffel against a Dutch airfield on an island in the mouth of the Rhein River. Since it was not quite light at 0545 we took off one at a time using our landing lights to form up. We flew at about 2000 meters in order to be above machine gun and small arms fire—there was no question about a fight this time, we were not going to be welcomed as liberators. As we approached our target all was quiet but we could see that the airfield was covered with all sorts of obstacles, trucks, old cars and even buses were scattered over the field effectively preventing any German aircraft from landing—but also preventing any defenders from taking off. We peeled off and strafed everything in sight, the few general aviation aircraft parked along the tarmac were left burning, but little permanent damage was done. On the return trip we still didn't encounter any enemy fighter opposition, but we did see wave after wave of our own fighters, bombers and transports on their way to the Rotterdam area. Our next mission was to Rotterdam, flying top cover for our paratroopers holding the bridges across the Nieuwe Maas River then return, rearm, refuel and off again, this time to the Hague area. We flew 3 to 4 missions each day, from sunrise to sunset.

I/ZG 1 intercepted six Blenheim IVs of RAF 600 Squadron over Walhaven airfield, five were shot down with only one escaping. Falck describes his experiences as he tries to bag the one that escaped.

I was on patrol in the area of the Hague when I spotted a Blenheim and tried to catch him. I chased him around church spires, around sand dunes, around trees, round and round we went only 10-15 meters high. I was right behind him but couldn't get a shot at him. When he broke for the open sea I thought 'Now I'll get him!' I began closing in on him but after a few kilometers he began circling a

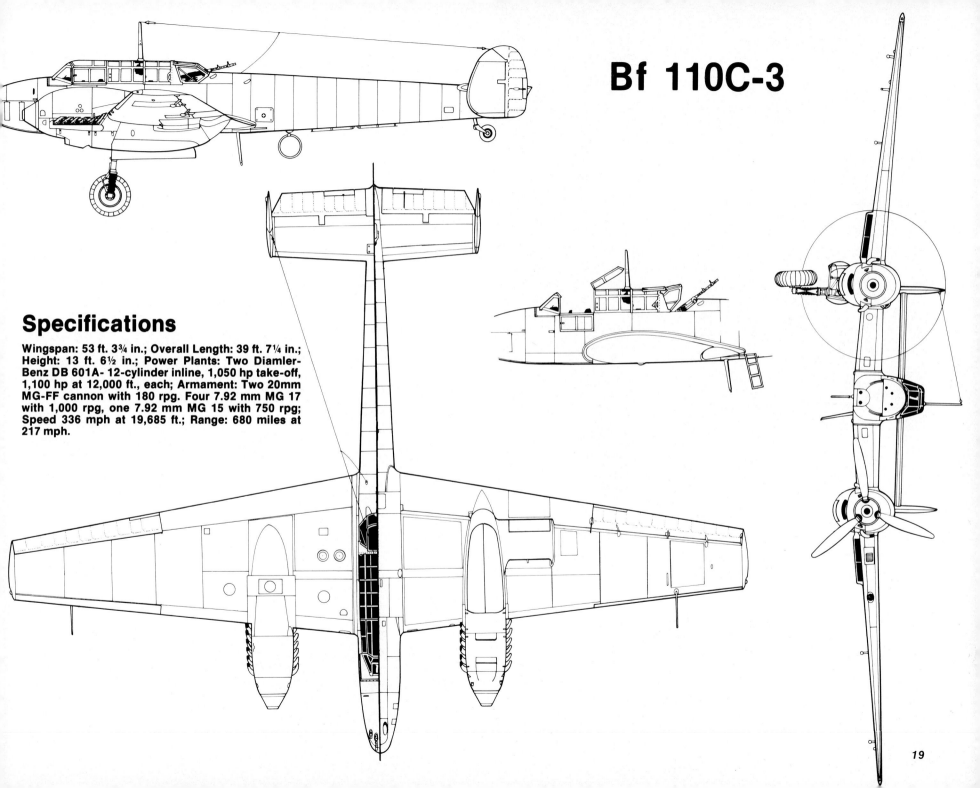

Bf 110C-3

Specifications

Wingspan: 53 ft. 3¾ in.; Overall Length: 39 ft. 7¼ in.; Height: 13 ft. 6½ in.; Power Plants: Two Diamler-Benz DB 601A- 12-cylinder inline, 1,050 hp take-off, 1,100 hp at 12,000 ft., each; Armament: Two 20mm MG-FF cannon with 180 rpg. Four 7.92 mm MG 17 with 1,000 rpg, one 7.92 mm MG 15 with 750 rpg; Speed 336 mph at 19,685 ft.; Range: 680 miles at 217 mph.

Oberleutnant Falck, now Kommandeur of I/ZG 1, greets General Kesselring at Kirchheim just before the invasion of France and the low countries. [Wolfgang Falck]

[Above Right] ZG 52 prepares to take off in the morning haze of 10 May against targets in France. One of the last units to receive their Bf 110s before the air battle of France, the lighter camouflage pattern on the fuselage is already evident. [Smithsonian Institution]

Lifting off into the bright mid-morning sunlight for their second mission against targets in Holland and Belgium, the machines of III/ZG 26 "Horst Wessel" sport mixed camouflage. [Bundesarchiv]

steamship at only a few meters above the waves. Round and round the ship and I couldn't get a shot at him. Finally he again broke for the open sea toward England but now I was low on fuel and had to break off my chase. The last I saw of him he was skimming the waves as fast as he could toward home. That Englishman was some pilot.

After five days of heavy fighting the Dutch Armed Forces capitulated and I/ZG 1 was sent south to join the battle of France.

In the South, II/ZG 76 had been flying top cover and strike missions in support of Army Group A's advance through Belgium and Luxembourg. Airfields were so crowded that for the first three days II/ZG 76 had to stage from Köln/Bonn airfield to Elsenborn, refuel and then fly into battle, usually not arriving over the front lines before 0900. On the second day of the invasion, 12 May, Leutnant Hans-Joachim Jabs of 6./ZG 76 was flying a strike mission in support of 4. Panzer Division when he got his first kill:

Your first girl you never forget and so it is quite the same with your first victory. We were about 3500 meters above the fortress at Namur in Belgium. It was good weather, not even any clouds. All of a sudden our Gruppen Kommandeur, Hauptmann Groth, goes down in a steep dive. I thought he was diving to strafe the fortress when I see two Curtiss Hawks on his tail. It was my first combat and I was too amazed to do anything except sit there with my mouth open. Then another flashes by me with his guns still blazing. Looking up I see one a little higher than me who turns and comes at me. I lift my nose and accelerate. Nose to nose we fire at each other. My four machine guns and twin cannon take its toll - he begins to burn as he slides along my left side and goes down. Banking around I watch him crash into the ground. I got my first kill! The next day I got a Morane and on the 15th of May I bagged two Moranes.

We no longer stage from Köln/Bonn to Elsenborn, but now begin to hop across the French country side right behind the Panzers, from one grassy meadow to another. No airfields, just cleared meadows. I'm looking for my fifth kill but it doesn't come. We've shot up the French Air Force and the Wehrmacht has overrun their bases. Everytime we see them they scatter.

With the French Air Force crippled, the Luftwaffe was now thrown almost completely into the tactical support of the advancing ground forces, although a constant effort was made to complete the destruction of the French and English Air Forces in France by continually carrying out low level surprise attacks. By the 20th the Germans had formed a bridgehead across the Somme and then swung north taking Boulogne and encircling Calais on the 29th. The British Expeditionary Forces were effectively encircled. On 26 May the British had begun falling back toward Dunkirk as the German armed forces tightened the noose around them. But in order to conserve his armor for later operations, von Rundstedt ordered the Panzers to halt their advance. The Luftwaffe was at the same time ordered to step up their attack. Göring boasted that he could destroy the British forces at Dunkirk from the air and prevent their being evacuated. On the 29th of May, Leutnant Hans-Joachim Jabs, having remained scoreless since his 4th victory on the 15th, was with his staffel over Dunkirk:

Fires were raging all over the city, our Stukas and Heinkels were really pounding it. Two comrades and I had just come through a huge cloud of oily smoke when all of a sudden several Spitfires are in front of us. Out of reflex I hit my firing buttons and two of them go down. One of the Tommies hits the parachute but I don't see if the other pilot got out before his airplane hit the ground. I had not only my fifth victory, but my sixth victory as well.

It was over Dunkirk however, that we pilots realized that our **110s** were not all we thought them to be. Until Dunkirk we Zerstörer were the elite, but when we at last met the Spitfire, we began taking large losses. We were too slow and not maneuverable enough. When we encountered Spitfires, they would turn into us and attack, one after the other, firing their eight machine guns and then roll over us and then turn and come back at us again. They were like bees and our cockpits were without armour protection. During the Battle of France our Gruppe lost 6 machines, but I believe most of them were to Spitfires over Dunkirk.

The action over Dunkirk did much to shake the confidence that the Zerstörer pilots had in their Bf 110s. For the first time the Luftwaffe's elite had come up against large numbers of Spitfires and Hurricanes when the RAF put up a maximum effort to provide an air umbrella over their evacuation fleet. By 4 June the British had evacuated 338,226 men including 120,000 French troops. In the four days from 27 May to 30 May British fighters claimed 179 Luftwaffe aircraft for a loss of only 29 fighters.

[Top] A formation of Bf 110Cs belonging to I/ZG 2 head out over the front line to strafe the retreating French forces. Now concerned less in hiding their aircraft on the ground the Zerstörer units began to lighten the colors applied to the sides of their aircraft as evidenced by the lead machine. [Bundesarchiv]

[Above] Finding their target, the Bf 110s of I/ZG 2 begin to roll into a dive. The massive nose armament of two 20 mm MG FF cannon with 180r.p.g. and four 7.9mm MG 17 machine guns with 1000r.p.g. proved devastating against all but heavily fortified ground targets. [Smithsonian Institution]

After the British evacuation of Dunkirk the Luftwaffe was able to turn its full attention to the task of finishing off the French Air Force and performing ground attack in support of the Army. On 10 June, Italy declared war on France and on the 12th Paris was declared an open city. Ten days later, on 22 June, Marshal Petain accepted German terms. Even before the end of hostilities in France, however, the Luftwaffe was already testing the Royal Air Force over the Channel by attacking British shipping.

To protect their shipping in the Channel the RAF put Hurricanes and Spitfires up in force, taking a deadly toll of the German bombers and their escorts. Oberleutnant Wolfgang Falck, Gruppen Kommandeur of I/ZG 1 describes the potentcy of the defenders while leading his stabschwarm on an escort mission over the channel.

It was the worst mission we had. I was the only one to come back and my machine had over 40 holes in it, my aircraft was so shot up I had to hold the stick in both hands. We were escorting bombers attacking shipping along the coast of England. In the distance we could see the Spitfires climbing to get altitude and position on us but we couldn't go after them since we had to stay with the bombers and wait for the Tommies to attack. When they did it was a slaughter - we just weren't maneuverable or fast enough to dogfight with them. There was nothing we could do, my comrades were falling in flames all around me. After being sprayed by gunfire several times I dove for the water with a Spitfire right on my tail. Flying so low I was almost hitting the waves I headed for the French Coast with my machine almost out of control: weaving back and forth and I tried to gain some height so we could bail out but every time I came up a little, a stream of tracers went by. My cannons were empty so I couldn't fight back even if I could get into position to fire. I kept yelling at my bordfunker to reload, but he couldn't. Pressed in the corner with four or five Gs pulling on him from my zigzagging, he could do little except fire sporadically at the Spitfires. As long as I kept close to the water the Tommies couldn't hit me but I didn't know how long I could keep my crate in the air; my throttle was shot out and fuel was streaming out of holes in my wings.

Finally I crossed the coast line and started dodging around sand dunes, houses and trees but they stayed right behind me, but not able to hit me. Not knowing how long I could keep my machine in the air I wanted to pull up and bail out, but every time I gained a little altitude tracers would go whizzing by. Crack! Something snapped in my wing, "...it's going to be a miracle if I can keep this off the ground!" I said aloud. Heading north with my escort still on my tail I flew right on the ground toward St. Trond. All of a sudden in front of my machine was a raised road with a British soldier riding along on a bicycle, his flat little helmet silhouetted against the sky. He was riding along probably thinking of his wife or girl friend when he glances to his right and sees me coming right at him. He rode his bicycle right off the road into mid-air as I pulled up to miss him. No tracers, the Spits were gone. After being so close to death I began laughing, thinking about the look on the Tommies face, laughing so hard I almost lost control of the aircraft. I could almost hear what the poor bicycle rider must have been thinking. 'The whole bloody German Air Force making a ground attack against one lonely bicycle rider'.

When I set down at St. Trond, General Kesselring was there. Pale and shaken, I must have been a sight because years and years later when I met Kesselring he said 'Hello, Falck, do you remember when you came back from that mission at St. Trond?'

At the end of June, Gruppen Kommandeur Falck, along with the second and third Staffel of I/ZG 1, was transferred to Düsseldorf for night fighter training, the staffeln being renamed I/NJG 1. The first staffel remained behind to become the nucleus of II/SKG 210.'

*The Whole tragic story of the German Night Fighter Force will be covered in **Nachtjagd**, a future Squadron/Signal release by Jerry L. Campbell.

Staying as close behind the front lines as possible the Zerstörergruppen hopped from one grassy field to another as the Panzers pushed the front lines forward. This fenced cow pasture occupied by II/ZG 76 is typical of these fields. [Bundesarchiv] [Smithsonian Institution]

II/ZG 76 over the smoking rubble of Dunkirk. The Bf 110, for the first time, met large numbers of modern single engine aircraft when the RAF put forth maximum effort to protect the evacuation of Allied troops.

The Battle of France created a number of new aces but more importantly it battle-seasoned the Luftwaffe for the coming campaigns. The above machines belong to 5./ZG 26. [Bundesarchiv]

These air frame mechanics are examining the tail assembly after it has taken hits from ground fire. Previously repaired damage can be seen on the rudder. Damage such as this usually caused few problems and could often times be repaired within an hour. [Bundesarchiv]

Main Landing Gear

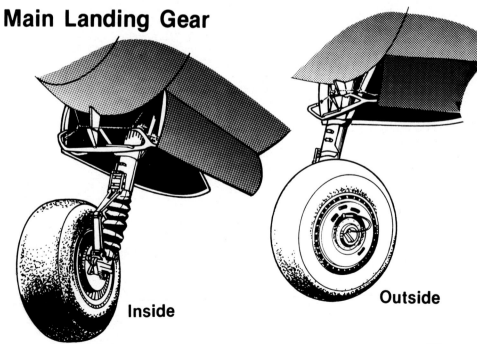

Inside

Outside

Bf 110D Long Range Zerstörer

The fighting in Norway and in particular the experiences of I/ZG 76 had revealed the need for increasing the operational range of the Bf 110, this coupled with the need to escort shipping in the North Sea against British air attack gave the development of a langstrecken (long range) Zerstörer the highest priority. A 264 Imp. gal. belly tank was fitted to the Bf 110. Fabricated from plywood and covered with fabric the tank in theory was to be dropped immediately after its contents were used up or enemy contact was made. First issued to 2. and 3./ZG 76 for patrol use in the North Sea these staffeln began losing aircraft in unexplained circumstances. It was later learned that even though the fuel was used up the tank was filled with highly volatile fumes and the tank had a tendency to hang up in low temperatures and sometimes explode.

Bf 110D-O Prototype - using Bf 110C-3 air frames several machines were adopted to accept the 264 Imp. Gal. belly tank in order to carry out service trials.

Bf 110D-1/R-1 Langstrecken Zerstörer - production version of the Langstrecken Zerstörer which shared the assembly line with the C series, the belly tank modification being made during final assembly.

Bf 110D-1/R2 Langstrecken Zerstörer - when the cause of the losses of the Bf 110D-1/R1 aircraft was attributed to the belly tank provisions were made for a pair of 198 Imp. gal. drop tanks under the outboard wings.

Bf 110D-2 Langstrecken Zerstörer - could carry a pair of 66 Imp. gal. jettisonable drops under the wings and mounted an ETC 500 bomb rack for carrying two 1,102 lb. bombs.

Bf 110D-3 Langstrecken Zerstörer - was capable of carrying either a pair of 66 Imp. gal. drop tanks or a pair of 198 Imp. gal. drop tanks. In addition the tail of the fuselage was lengthened to provide space for a rubber dingy. An ETC 500 bomb rack was optional.

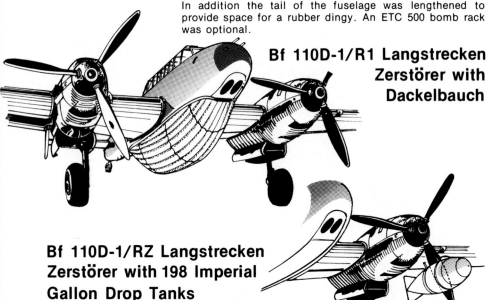

Bf 110D-1/R1 Langstrecken Zerstörer with Dackelbauch

Bf 110D-1/RZ Langstrecken Zerstörer with 198 Imperial Gallon Drop Tanks

The D-1/R1 shared the assembly lines with the C-Series, being run simultaneously.

A Bf 110D-1/R1 with the Dackelbauch is prepared for a flight from Aalborg. The huge jettisonable belly tanks were found to hang up at low temperatures and due to inadequate ventilation volatile gasses would remain in the tank sometimes exploding.

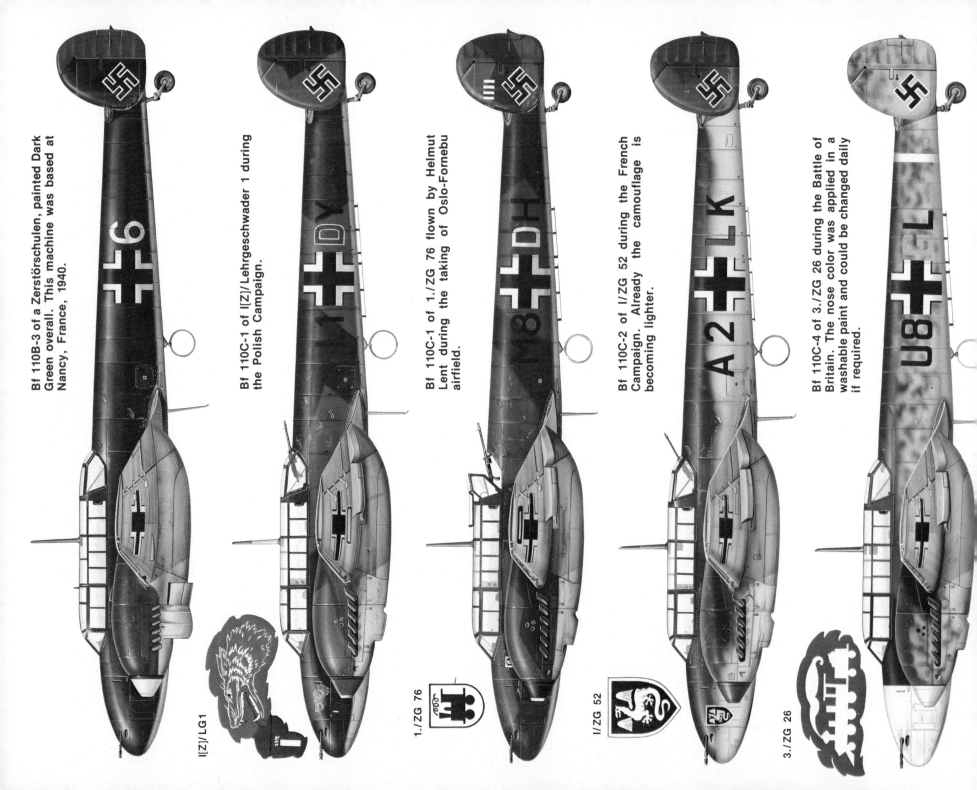

Bf 110B-3 of a Zerstörschulen, painted Dark Green overall. This machine was based at Nancy, France, 1940.

I(Z)/LG1

Bf 110C-1 of I(Z)/Lehrgeschwader 1 during the Polish Campaign.

1./ZG 76

Bf 110C-1 of 1./ZG 76 flown by Helmut Lent during the taking of Oslo-Fornebu airfield.

I/ZG 52

Bf 110C-2 of I/ZG 52 during the French Campaign. Already the camouflage is becoming lighter.

3./ZG 26

Bf 110C-4 of 3./ZG 26 during the Battle of Britain. The nose color was applied in a washable paint and could be changed daily if required.

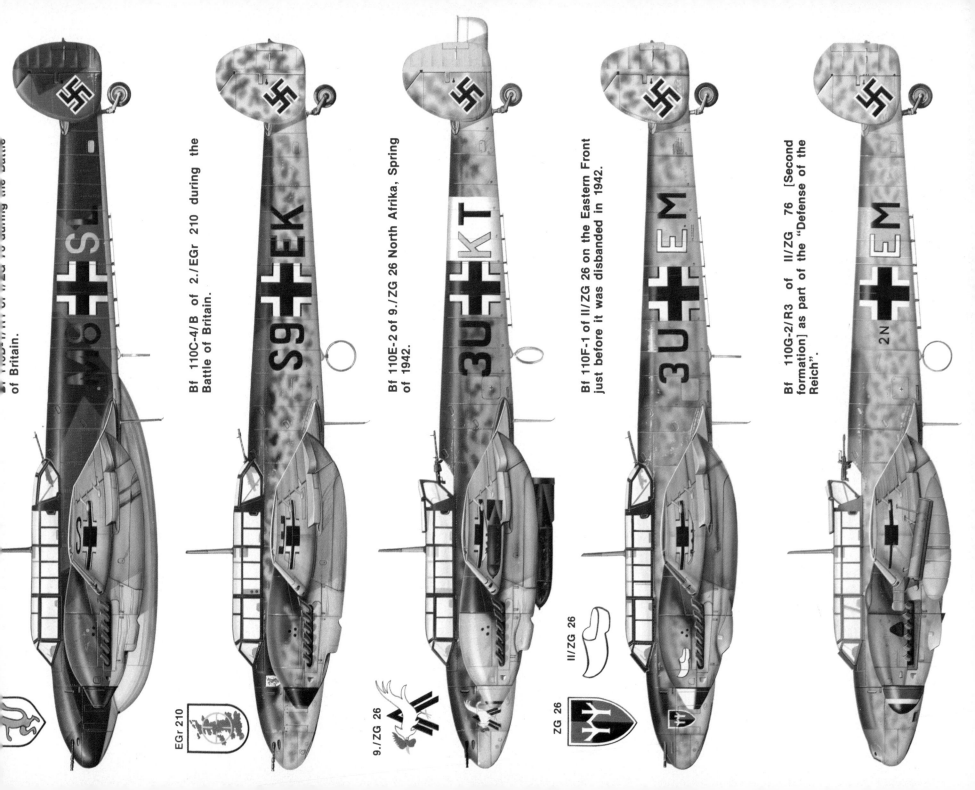

Bf 110D-1/R1 of I./ZG 76 during the Battle of Britain.

Bf 110C-4/B of 2./EGr 210 during the Battle of Britain.

EGr 210

Bf 110E-2 of 9./ZG 26 North Afrika, Spring of 1942.

9./ZG 26

Bf 110F-1 of II/ZG 26 on the Eastern Front just before it was disbanded in 1942.

II/ZG 26

ZG 26

Bf 110G-2/R3 of II/ZG 76 [Second formation] as part of the "Defense of the Reich".

Battle of Britain

Just forty-six days after it had begun the campaign in the West was over. Holland, Belgium, Luxembourg and France had each been defeated and conquered, Great Britain had been thrown back across the channel. The war was won! The Wehrmacht's Panzers had crushed the mightest armies Europe could muster against them, and the Luftwaffe had destroyed the best that the Allied air forces could put in the air; Göring's elite, the Zerstörer, had performed admirably, clearing the air and ground of enemy aircraft when and wherever they could be found. Only the RAF, licking its wounds across the channel was between Germany and complete victory in the West. Since the end of the fighting in France, Hitler had made several lightly veiled peace overtures to Great Britain hoping that further fighting between the two countries could be averted. Each of these had been rejected out of hand by 10 North Downing.

As these peace feelers were put out, the Luftwaffe, supremely confident in its ability to destroy the RAF, was resting and replacing losses after the previous six weeks of heavy fighting. Newer models of the Bf 110 were now entering service, the Bf 110D 'Langstrecken Zerstörer' had reached 2. and 3./ZG 76 and were already carrying out long-range shipping patrols along the Norwegian coast. The Bf 110C-4s with the addition of armour protection for the air crew was beginning to replace the unarmoured C-1s, 2s and 3s in Zerstörergruppen. Bf 110C-4/B Jabos (fighter/bombers) equipped with a pair of ETC 250 bomb racks under the fuselage were arriving at the Channel coast equipping Erprobungsgruppe 210, an experimental unit set up to work out suitable fighter-bomber tactics. The various Aufklärungsstaffeln were receiving the Bf 110C-5 and operating them in mixed units alongside of other reconnaissance aircraft.

French and British equipment was pressed into immediate service whenever found. Here a small French munitions carrier is used to tow an aircraft belonging to I/ZG 52. [Smithsonian Institution]

After the ordeal in France of constant flying and fighting, the Zerstörergruppen spent the weeks before the coming Battle of Britain completely overhauling their aircraft. [Bundesarchiv]

A proud Hans-Joachim Jabs, now a veteran with six victories, poses on the wing of his shark mouthed Zerstörer while it is being refueled just before the Battle of Britain began. [Hans-Joachim Jabs]

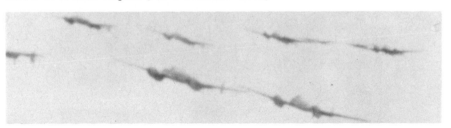

Massed Zerstörer formations protecting the bombers figured heavily in the Luftwaffe's plan to subjugate and eventually destroy the RAF. The machines of II/ZG 76 practice formation flying during July 1940 just prior to the assault on Great Britain. [Hans-Joachim Jabs]

While all this reequipping was going on, the Luftwaffe was ordered 'to close the Channel to enemy shipping' and consequently RAF bases in England were attacked only sporadically. However the attacks on Channel shipping brought up large numbers of British fighters with which the Luftwaffe came to grips. Since the British Government had rejected his peace proposals even to the point of ridiculing them, Hitler issued orders that the 'Arrogant Island' should be brought to its knees through seaborn invasion. Before this could be carried out, however, the Luftwaffe had to first eliminate the Royal Air Force and then strangle the seaborne supply of Great Britain by attacking its ports and shipping. The last phase would be the air support of the invasion fleet itself.

The elimination of the RAF was to be accomplished by destroying those fighter defenses south of a line between London and Gloucester and then moving the line progressively northward until the U.K. was purged of fighter opposition. To carry out this task the Luftwaffe massed some 2600 aircraft along the French, Belgium, Dutch and Norwegian coasts. Of these aircraft poised along the Channel and in Denmark and Norway were 289 Bf 110C's and D's in the following units:

E.Gr. 210*	Bf 110C-4Bs and Bf 109 Fighter/bombers
1./ZG 1**	Bf 110C-1s and Bf 110C-4/Bs
I,II/ZG 2***	Bf 110Cs
I,II/ZG 76	Bf 110C-4s and D-1s
I,II,III/ZG 26	Bf 110s
V(Z)/LG 1****	Bf 110C-4s and D-1s

*By the end of the Battle of Britain this unit would be renamed SKG 210.
**1./ZG 1 would shortly become II/SKG 210.
***II/ZG 2 was formed from I/ZG 52.
****Formerly I(Z)/LG 1.

ETC 250 Racks

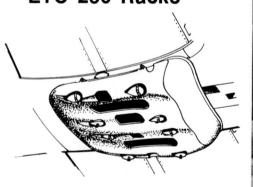

In order to further increase the versatility of his Zerstörer, Messerschmitt developed the Jabo version. Powered by a pair of increased horsepower DB 601N engines, the Bf 110C-4/B was equipped with paired ETC 250 racks on the center line capable of carrying a pair of 551 lb. bombs. [Bundesarchiv]

The Bf 110C-4/B fighter-bomber was first delivered to Erprobungsgruppe 210, an experimental unit, which began operations against British Channel shipping during July 1940. E.Gr. 210's 1st and 2nd Staffel were equipped with Bf 110 Jabos while the 3rd Staffel was equipped with Bf 109 Jabos. [Bundesarchiv]

The Zerstörer pilots at the time of the Battle of Britain were nearly all battle tested veterans, and a number of them were already aces. [Bundesarchiv]

III/ZG 26 was the first Zerstörer unit to engage British fighters over England when on 9 July they were part of a mixed Bf 109 and Bf 110 escort force protecting He 111s and Ju 88s attacking a convoy in the mouth of the Thames. The defending Hurricanes downed one Bf 110. Note that this standard fighter has the DB 601N engines signified by the white N on the engine cowlings. [Bundesarchiv]

Since a good deal of the area south of the Gloucester-London line was beyond the range of the Bf 109, the Bf 110s would be used extensively to escort and protect the bomber formations. The attack plan called for the Zerstörer to use their endurance to lead the attack bringing up and engaging the defenders until they had exhausted their fuel. As the British single engine machines were landing to rearm and refuel, the bombers with another flight of protective Bf 110s would arrive and attack the airfields now covered with helpless fighters. A plan designed to cripple the RAF during the first major encounter.

Unfortunately for the plan, the Bf 110s were nearly incapable of defending themselves against the Hurricanes and Spitfires. When this type of raid was carried out, the initial Zerstörer were routed, those not shot down or heavily damaged were sent fleeing for the coast. The second wave Bf 110s flying escort with the bombers then found themselves forced into a defensive circle long before the bombers had reached their target. Before long Bf 109s had to be assigned to protect the Zerstörer as well as the bombers.

Sporadic raids had been carried out against targets in the Channel and on ports throughout the month of July and early August. On the 6 August Göring called his Generals together to outline his plan, "Adlerangriff" (Attack of the Eagles), for the air offensive against the RAF. The opening attack, under the code name Adlertag (Eagle Day), was to be a massed attack against RAF bases on 10 August. In fact the weather turned bad and

Hptm. Rettberg, Kommandeur of II/ZG 26, briefs his air crew before a sortie over England. Many of these men would not return from sorties against RAF Fighter Command, after being shot down and either killed or captured. [Bundesarchiv]

Flying out over the Channel for their first raid on English soil, the Zerstörergruppen, if somewhat shaken by their experience against Hurricanes and Spitfires in France, were still confident of the final outcome of the battle. The RAF would be destroyed and Britain would be subjugated. [Bundesarchiv]

remained so on the 10th and 11th postponing Adlertag until the 13th.

Monday 12 August dawned bright and clear. Probing the British defenses during the previous month had demonstrated the effectiveness of the British radar system. So the experimental Jabo unit, E.Gr.210, was assigned the task of destroying all known radar stations between Portland and the Thames Estuary. With 551 lb. bombs slung beneath their fuselage Hauptmann Walter Rubensdörfer led his Gruppe, 1. and 2. Staffel equipped with Bf 110C-4/Bs and 3. Staffel equipped with Bf 109E-4/Bs to the coast of England where they split up to attack their individual targets. Although in each case the attacks were brilliantly executed all of the stations except one were back in operation within a few hours. After E.Gr.210 returned to report the success of their mission a force consisting of nearly a hundred Ju 88s of KG 51 protected by one hundred and twenty Bf 110s of ZG 2 and ZG 76 and twenty-five Bf 109Es of JG 53 tookoff. Not picked up on radar until the raiding force was nearing their targets, Portsmouth and Ventnor on the Isle of Wright were heavily bombed, 10 Ju 88s being lost to British fighters.

Shortly after the KG 51 raid, E.Gr.210 swept across Manston airfield strafing and bombing. Lasting only a few minutes, the attackers left the British air field looking like what they thought was a carnage of burning wreckage. In fact the Spitfires of 65 Squadron were only slightly damaged and one of the Bf 110s was shot down by a Spitfire of 54 Squadron. Five Bf 110s were lost on this day.

13 August — Adlertag

At 0500, 74 Do 17s of KG 2 headed for the French coast where they were to meet their escort, sixty Bf 110s of ZG 76. Unbeknownst to the bombers the raid had been cancelled because of weather and their protective fighters had been recalled. Five Dorniers were shot down and five were damaged. Shortly before noon, I/ZG 2, now led by Hauptmann Heinlein since Major Ott was shot down and killed by a Spitfire of 609 Squadron a few days before, took off. This raid also had been postponed due to weather but ZG 2 had not been informed. Not meeting their bombers the Zerstörer pushed on to Portland where they tangled with Spitfires losing one aircraft. The first really big raid came during the middle of the afternoon when thirty Zerstörer of V(Z)/LG 1 escorting 120 Ju 88s were part of a larger attacking force. V(Z)/LG 1 lost four Bf 110s out of a total of fourteen Zerstörer lost on

Adlertag. The day was something less than a success and provided a fleeting glimpse of the disaster that was just two days away.

15 August — Black Thursday

The next day, E.Gr.210s Bf 110C-4/Bs again struck at Manston losing two machines to ground fire. After the fiasco of Adlertag and a relatively quiet day on the 14th, the Zerstörer were in heavy combat on the 15th. In the North, Luftflotte 5 launched its first large scale attack from Norway and Denmark. Twenty-one Dackelbauch (Daschhund-belly) equipped Bf 110D-1/R1s of I/ZG 76 based at Aalborg met their charges, seventy He 111s of I and II/KG 26 from Stavanger, over the North Sea. Hoping that the heavy attacks in the South had tied up most of the fighters, the RAF bases of Dishforth and Linton-On-Ouse were to be attacked. Unknown to German intelligence, a strong reserve of fighters had been kept in the North for just such an event. At 1345, while the raiders were still some twenty-five miles out to sea, the radar directed Spitfires of No. 72 Squadron attacked out of the sun. The first plane to be hit was the machine belonging to ZG 76's Gruppenkommandeur, Hauptmann Restemeyer, which exploded when the unreleased Dackelbauch was penetrated, and seconds later, the Gruppe adjutant's aircraft was seen to go down as did a Heinkel. A wild melee of individual air battles took place as the Langstrecken Zerstörer vainly tried to defend the bombers and wound up fighting for their own existence. Five minutes later, the Hurricanes of 605 Squadron dived to the attack. After losing nearly a third of their number, I/ZG 76 was forced to flee for Denmark, leaving the bombers to their own devices. After taking such heavy losses, Luftflotte 5 never again launched a large scale raid, and in September, I/ZG 76 was withdrawn from the Battle and retrained as a night fighter unit.

Meanwhile in the south, 16 Bf 110s and Bf 109s of E.Gr.210 attacked Martlesham in a low level raid that knocked the airfield out for nearly two days. At about 1730, forty Bf 110s of ZG 2 escorting sixty Ju 88s of LG 1 were intercepted by four squadrons of British fighters. Downing one Bf 110 the interceptors were able to force their way to the bombers, knocking down eight of them. At 1820, Rubensdörfer again led his E.Gr. 210 to the attack, this time against RAF Kenley. Having missed his Bf 109 escort the attack was pursued anyway, in the event against RAF Croyden due to an error in navigation. As before under Rubensdörfer, the attack was a success, destroying a number of buildings including a factory engaged in the repair of Hurricanes. As E.Gr. 210 broke off their raid Hurricanes swept in on them. Initially going into a defensive circle, the Bf 110s suddenly broke for cloud cover. As they did, the Stab flight came under attack and Rubensdörfer's aircraft went down billowing smoke. Including their Kommandeur, E.Gr. 210 lost six Bf 110s and one Bf 109. Other actions over England cost II/ZG 76 Haifischgruppe, eight Bf 110s and III/ZG 76 lost three. Of the 83 odd machines lost by the Luftwaffe on this day twenty-six (31%) were from the Zerstörergruppen.

On Friday the 16th, the Zerstörergruppen lost an additional eight machines, half of them from ZG 76. Almost no sorties were flown on the 17th despite good weather. The 18th of August, however, again brought the Luftwaffe to the attack and it was the turn of ZG 26 to get chewed up, losing fourteen machines in a single day. By now it was becoming increasingly obvious that the Bf 110 could not hold its own in combat with the British single seat fighters. At a meeting on the 19th, however, Göring

would listen to no criticism of his Bf 110, blaming instead the leadership of some of his senior commanders or the imcompetence of the pilots. He did issue orders that henceforth Bf 109s were to be detailed to fly close escort for the Zerstörergruppen. Even so it was not until the 25th that the Bf 110s returned to the battle, with I and II/ZG 2, and V(Z)/LG 1 escorting II/KG 51 and II/KG 54 in an attack against Portland, Weymouth and Warmwell. Despite the presence of Bf 109s from "Pik As", ZG 2 lost six machines and V(Z)/LG 1 lost two. On 26 August, only two machines were lost despite the fact over 100 Bf 110s were put over England. The 28th saw sixty Bf 110s over England without a loss. The Bf 109 escort was paying off. On the afternoon of the 29th, 500 Bf 109s and 150 Bf 110s escorted a small number of bombers hoping to entice Fighter Command up to fight. The ploy went without results.

During the month of August over 120 Bf 110s were lost and it had now become obvious, even to Göring, that the Zerstörer could not hold its own against the nimble British fighters. Unfortunately, because of a shortage of single engine machines the Zerstörergruppen could not be withdrawn from the battle but their role was curtailed.

September

Monday, 2 September, saw nine Zerstörer lost, four from ZG 2, three from ZG 26 and two from ZG 76. On 3 September 80 Bf 110s of ZG 2 and ZG 26 escorted fifty-four Dorniers of KG 2 attacking North Weald airfields. Although somewhat slow to react, the British ground controllers vectored 1, 17, 19, 46, 249, 257, 310 and part of 603 Squadron onto the raiders as they left the target. Fighting tenaciously the Bf 110s were able to protect their charges, losing only one Do 17Z, but ZG 2 lost five machines and ZG 26 lost four machines. The next day the Zerstörergruppen, now with one staffel each equipped C-4/B fighter bombers, carried out a number of low level attacks covered by their own twin engine fighters. Sixteen Bf 110s, including one from E.Gr. 210 which lost it's second GruppenKommandeur, Hptm. von Boltenstern shot down by Hurricanes of 601 Squadron, were lost. After suffering no losses on the 5th, four Bf 110s were lost on the 6th.

The Battle of London Begins

On the 7th, Göring personally took command and launched a massive attack on London with 348 bombers escorted by over 600 fighters. The only Zerstörergruppen included in the force was ZG 2. In a mass, over one and one half miles high and covering 800 square miles, the huge armada flew up the Thames Estuary toward London. As the bombers approached London twenty-one Squadrons of British fighters ripped into them. At 1745 the first wave of bombers headed for home and at 2010 the second wave began its attack. The Battle of Britain had now shifted from RAF airfields to London—the Battle of Britain had been lost and the Battle of London had begun. For such a large raid the Zerstörer losses were light, only seven Bf 110s were lost, all from ZG 2. The second day of the attack on London was quiet with no Zerstörer being lost on this day. Night attacks, which had begun earlier, were unceasing however, and were now becoming more important than the daylight attacks. On the 9th, four Bf 110s of ZG 76 were lost in sporadic raids and none on the 10th. The 11th brought increased daylight activity costing the Zerstörergruppen nine Bf 110s. The 12th and 13th and 14th were quiet with little daylight activity and no Zerstörer losses.

On the 15th the Luftwaffe returned in mass and losses were heavy among the bombers but only three Bf 110s belonging to LG 1 were lost. Bad weather on the 16th kept the Luftwaffe on the ground with only a few sorties being carried out. The Zerstörergruppen carried out few missions during the next few days and lost no aircraft. On the 24th, the new Gruppen Kommandeur of E.Gr.210 led eighteen Bf 110 fighter-bombers of his 1st and 2nd Staffel escorted by Bf 110 fighters of ZG 76 on an attack against a factory along the coast. One machine of E.Gr. 210 and four machines of ZG 76 were lost to flak. The 25th cost the Zerstörergruppen five more Bf 110s. On the 26th seventy Zerstörer of ZG 26 escorted Heinkels on an attack at the Woolston aircraft factory at Southampton. Two of the Zerstörer were lost.

The 27th dawned bright and clear and at 0815, six flights of Bf 110 fighter bombers of V(Z)/LG 1 and II/ZG 76 began hit and run attacks as far north as London followed by Ju 88s of KG 77 which suffered heavy losses. Before noon E.Gr. 210 escorted by nearly thirty Bf 110s of III/ZG 26 attacked the Bristol Factory. Bf 110 losses were heavy, nineteen Zerstörer were lost and the 3rd Gruppen Kommandeur of E.Gr. 210 was killed and the crack Jabo unit also lost its fourth Staffelkapitän. As it turned out this was to be the last raid which the Zerstörergruppen would participate in large numbers. In order to replace losses, ZG 2 was disbanded and the planes and personnel were passed to other units. During the month of October, ZG 76 was withdrawn from the battle. ZG 26 continued to soldier on in the battle but at great cost. On 7 October II and III ZG 26 lost seven machines while escorting twenty-five Ju 88s on a raid against the Westland Aircraft factory. After this, even the participation of ZG 26 was curtailed as the Luftwaffe went over almost exclusively to the night bombing role. Those surviving Zerstörergruppen were now dispersed to undergo a much needed rest and reequipment. Never again would the Zerstörergruppen occupy the place of honor they had before the Battle of Britain.

ZG 26 was led by the wooden-legged veteran Oberstleutnant Joachim Huth. I Gruppe was based at Yurench, II Gruppe at Crecy, and III Gruppe at Barleg. [Smithsonian Institution]

On 11 August, sixty-one Bf 110s of I and II/ZG2 were assigned to escort Ju 88s from KG 54 and He 111s of KG 27 on an attack against Portland. Additional fighter protection was provided by Bf 109s from JG 2. A massive dogfight between the escort and Hurricanes ensued in which sixteen Hurricanes, six Bf 110s, five Ju 88s, one He 111 and six Bf 109s were shot down. Unfortunately for ZG 2, Major Ott, Gruppen Kommandeur of I/ZG 2, was one of those that fell. [Bundesarchiv]

ZG 26's aircraft often had the nose painted in a frequently changed identification color. [Bundesarchiv]

5./ZG 26 over Tonbridge, Kent on 2 Sept. 1940, carrying out low level attacks. 3U+GN was shot down by British fighters with the pilot, Ofw. Rochel and his gunner Uffz. Schözler being posted as missing. [Bundesarchiv]

An extremely rare photograph taken by a fast thinking gunner who had just shot down an RAF Spitfire and then grabbed his camera. [Bundesarchiv]

Lehrgeschwader 1 [LG1] was a training and development Geschwader made up of former instructors and personnel of the prewar Technical Development Flying Unit and operationally attached to VIII Flieger Korps. V[Zerstörer]/LG 1 flew Bf 110s from Caen carrying the code L1 and a wolf's head on the nose. In October this unit was retrained as a Night Fighter Gruppe, being renamed I/NJG 3. [Bundesarchiv]

The 1st Staffel of ZG 26 "Horst Wessel" carried "Der Ringelpitz" a red outlined in white German alligator chasing a black outlined in white British fish. Both open mouths are red. [Bundesarchiv]

In the Fall of 1940, after heavy losses, ZG 52 was disbanded. Some of the aircraft and personnel were absorbed by ZG 26 as evidenced by the above photograph. The center machine has ZG 52's emblem showing through the washable color applied to the nose and the lighter band of color on the fuselage beneath the Geschwader codes also shows evidence of repainting. [Smithsonian Institution]

The Balkans and Greece

During October, as the Battle of Britain was winding down, Mussolini, piqued at Hitler's military successes decided on having a European adventure of his own and began delivering ultimatums to Greece. When these ultimatums were rejected, the Italians began on invasion of Greece from Albania on 28 October 1940. After some initial successes, the Italian attack was blunted and by 22 November, the Greek Army had begun to push the Italians back and after a winter of hard fighting almost half of Albania was in Greek hands. Fearing further British involvement, Hitler decided he must come to the aid of his southern ally by attacking Greece through Yugoslavia and Bulgaria after obtaining free passages through these countries. A coup in Yugoslavia thwarted these plans, so it was decided that both Yugoslavia and Greece would be subjugated by the Wehrmacht. On 6 April 1941, Germany launched the attack with 33 divisions supported by strong Luftwaffe formations. Meeting little fighter opposition, the Zerstörergruppen, I and II/ZG26 and II/ZG76 again became the elite, carrying out ground support and strike missions throughout the campaign. After only eleven days, the Yugoslavian government capitulated and by 26 April Greece had been overrun. Although the RAF and British land forces were committed, they could do little to stem the German juggernaut streaming across Greece.

The British managed to evacuate 43,000 men to Crete, although all heavy equipment and another 11,000 men were left behind. Realizing that Crete was a strategic threat to the successful occupation of his southern flank, Hitler ordered that the island must be captured, allocating one airborne division and one paratroop division.

On the morning of 20 May, the attack began. Both Gruppen of ZG 26 and II/ZG 76 took part in the invasion of Crete, flying escort and ground attack missions throughout the assault. The heavy nose armament of the Bf 110 was used as airborned artillery to support the beleaguered paratroopers who had run into stiff opposition on the ground. Suffering heavy losses, the Germans quickly gained control of the island. The British evacuated nearly 15,000 troops, but left behind 18,000 prisoners.

For a short time in May, 4./ZG 76 was detached to support the insurgents in Iraq with their Bf 110D-3s carrying Iraqi markings.

Bf 110s of ZG 26 seen high above the extremely mountainous terrain of the Balkans. Meeting little fighter opposition, the Zerstörer reigned supreme, carrying out air strikes at will with more losses through accidents than operations. [Gene Stafford]

The rough countryside in the Balkans provided ZG 26 plenty of material with which to camouflage their aircraft. When it was realized that there was almost no aircraft facing them, this toil was dispensed with. [Bundesarchiv]

Lined up on a forward airfield in Greece, the Bf 110D-3s of 4./ZG 76 Haifischgruppe present a lethal picture. The MG cover on the nose is white as are the tips of the spinner. [Lee Barlow]

Africa

In North Africa, things were also going badly for the Italians who were in full retreat in the face of a smaller British force. Visualizing British control of all Africa, Hitler decided to dispatch forces to prop up Mussolini's troops, at least enough to keep them from collapsing. The first unit to arrive was the Bf 110 equipped III./ZG 26, which was reinforced by 2. Staffel, arriving on 30 January 1941 and immediately dispersed to airfields at Castel Benito, Sirte and Arco Philenorum. Going into action quickly, the Zerstörer unit had lost six aircraft by the end of February while only having shot down two enemy machines.

At the end of March, Rommel struck, leading his forces against British lines forcing them to withdraw and beginning a retreat that would not stop until Rommel's forces were threatening Egypt itself. Flying against Hurricanes and Tomahawks over the open expanses of the desert where their range stood them well, the Bf 110s faired much better than they had against the RAF during missions across the Channel; through the end of August 1941, III/ZG 26 claimed some 33 enemy aircraft for a loss of only 23 Zerstörer.

Hans-Joachim Jabs banks his plane low over Argus on the Greek peninsula of Peloponnesus. By 28 April, the British had evacuated some 43,000 men from Peloponnesus before the Germans captured the port of Kalamata, but they left behind some 11,000 and all their heavy equipment. [Hans-Joachim Jabs]

Using 66 Imp. gal. drop tanks, II/ZG 76 carries out a patrol over Crete. By the time ZG 76 appeared over Crete, most of the RAF's strength had left the island leaving only a few Hurricanes and Gladiators to face the Luftwaffe. These were quickly subdued and when the Germans launched their invasion the only Allied air cover available had to fly from Egypt. [Hans-Joachim Jabs]

The first Luftwaffe units sent to North Africa were 2. and III/ZG 26 arriving at Arco Philenorum, Castel Benito and Sirte on 30 Jan. 1941 under the command of Gruppenkommandeur Major Karl Kaschka. [Smithsonian Institution]

For a short time immediately after their arrival in North Africa, 9./ZG 26 carried their staffel color, yellow, on the engine nacelles of their aircraft. The yellow extends onto the spinner which is tipped with a circle of black and then white. [Bundesarchiv]

Carburetor Intake

Dust Filter for Carburetor Intake

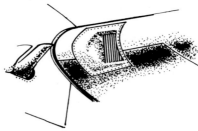

[Above Left] Some idea of the conditions in the desert can be seen in the great cloud of dust raised by the back wash from the propellers of the above Zerstörer. [Bundesarchiv]

The vast stretches of unbroken terrain allowed the Zerstörer, assigned to ground support, to stay very close to the ground troops using small forward airfields that could be made ready in hours. [Smithsonian Institution]

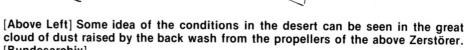

This Bf 110D-3 of 7./ZG 26 carrying the long range 198 Imp. gal. drop tanks sits on a Sicilian airfield after escorting Ju 52s returning from Africa. The very clearly seen "N" on the outboard nacelle denoted that the machine was powered by DB 601N engines and was to be fueled with 96 octane C3 fuel. [Bundesarchiv]

Flying top cover for convoys plying the Mediterranean was usually a long and monotonous task. Note the heavy demarcation line to the camouflage on the nose of the D-3 Zerstörer in the foreground. [Mihai Moisescu]

Barbarossa

At 0300 on 22 June 1941, the German Army began the invasion of Soviet Russia. Supported by a strong Luftwaffe, the attack was an immediate and stunning success, with the Panzer divisions knifing through Russian defenses to a depth of over two hundred miles during the first week. The Luftwaffe's primary task was the destruction of the Red Air Force. The first week brought the Luftwaffe unbelievable successes with claims mounting to over 6000 aircraft destroyed; and although these claims are still not completely confirmed, it is known that the Russian Military Air Power

Commander, Lieutenant-General Kopels, committed suicide on the second day when he had already lost 600 aircraft and could only claim 12 German aircraft. Since most of the Zerstörer equipped Gruppen that survived the Battle of Britain were either in North Africa with Rommel or undergoing night fighter conversion in order to combat the increasing RAF night raids on Germany, only the Bf 110 equipped Schnellkampfgeschwader 210* (SKG 210) and II/ZG 26 were available for Barbarossa.

Attached to Luftflotte 2 supporting Army Group Center, the Bf 110s while small in number, initially only some 60 aircraft, struck Soviet airbases in low level attacks. Finding the Russian airfields covered with aircraft parked in peacetime rows without camouflage, the Zerstörers streaked across their assigned airfields bombing and strafing everything in sight leaving behind little but burning hulks. The Luftwaffe attacked 31 airfields in the first wave, destroying hundreds of enemy machines and losing only two aircraft. The carnage went on hour after hour, day after day, complete air units were destroyed on the ground and the few Red machines that did get into the air were quickly dispatched. Because most of the destruction took place on the ground, however, comparatively few aircrew were lost, leaving the Soviets a large pool of personnel with which to begin rebuilding.

After the first few weeks the Soviet Air Force could offer only feeble resistance and the Bf 110s were able to go over to the low level attack role, carrying out strafing and bombing attacks on front lines, roads and railway lines. By 31 July, ZG 26 had put in claims for 620 enemy aircraft destroyed in low level attacks and aerial combat. On 19 August, ZG 26 was officially noted for having carried out two attacks on a Soviet airbase at Nizino south of Leningrad, destroying 15 and leaving 30 burning on the ground, and destroying 3 in the air, raising their score to 854 enemy machines including 191 in aerial combat. On 15 September, II/ZG 26 participated in Operations Beowulf I and II, the seaborn landings on the Baltic Islands of Muhu, Saaremaa and Hüumaa. Acting as flying artillery, the Bf 110s carried out 118 sorties losing only two machines. Between 22 June and 27 September, ZG 26 was credited with having shot down 96 aircraft, destroying 741 on the ground, destroying 148 tanks, 166 artillery pieces, 3,280 vehicles, 49 railroad trains, one armoured train, 68 locomotives and 4 bridges.

In the Northern Sector a schwarm of II/ZG 76 and I/JG 77 operated Bf 110s under Luftflotte 5 based at Oslo, Norway. Because of weather, it was not until 25 June that operations got underway with a strike at Niva, Varlamova and Vaenga airfields on which the Zerstörer were able to catch the Russian aircraft, three days after the war had begun, lined up wing tip to wing tip. Moving into Finland in order to shorten the distance to Murmansk, raids were carried out as often as time and weather permitted, with the Bf 110s also carrying out escort duties for the bombers. By 12 July, Hauptmann G. Schascke had claimed 12 kills and by 4 August he had his 20th kill but was shot down behind Russian lines. The coming of Fall however, saw the few machines of II ZG 76 being pulled from the Northern sector to undergo night fighter training, leaving only 7.(Z)/JG 5 operating twelve Bf 110s in Luftflotte 5.

In the south, I and II SKG 210 flew ground attack in support of Operation Taifun, an eveloping attack designed to destroy Army Group Timoshenko and open up the way to Moscow. The huge pincer movement

*Formerly E.Gr.210

Known as the "Clog Gruppe" because of their wooden shoe emblem, II/ZG 26, was part of the initial "Barbarrossa" force that invaded the Soviet Union. The Geschwader insignia can be seen on the nose of the machines with the Gruppe insignia on the cowling. [Bundesarchiv]

Oberstleutnant Schalk, Kommodore of ZG 26, carried his chevron just below the cockpit. Schalk led III/ZG 26 until November 1940, when he took over as Geschwader Kommodore of ZG 26. Withdrawn from the Battle of Britain, Schalk led his Geschwader into the Balkans and then into Russia. [Bundesarchiv]

The radio operator proudly poses beside the kill marked tail of the Bf 110E belonging to Wilhelm Spies, Kommandeur of I/ZG 26, on the East Front during fall of 1941. [Bundesarchiv]

Operating Bf 110C-4/B fighter-bombers, 7.[Z]/JG 5 carried out low level attacks against Russian airfields in the northern sector. The unit emblem was a Dachshund with a Russian I-16 "Rata" in its' mouth. [Ossi Anttonen]

LN + KR of 7.[Z]/JG 5 over the Finnish area of the Eastern Front. The camera was either equipped with awfully fast film or this unit found a way of saving fuel after becoming airborne. [Bundesarchiv]

The fall of 1941 saw a very early snow ushering in one of Russia's earliest and most severe winters on record. [Ossi Anttonen]

Although the Luftwaffe had nearly complete control of the skies and had little to fear from Russian fighters, the Russian Anti-Aircraft defense was a constant problem. Lieutnant N. Kulier, Commander of a Soviet A A battery poses beside his Bf 110 kill during early spring of 1942. Russian propaganda credited Kulier with 8 kills to date. [Russian News Services]

When 2. and 3. Staffeln of ZG 1 were transferred to the night fighters, 1/ZG 1 [Wespe] was used to form the fighter-bomber II Gruppe/SKG 210. Retaining their wasp emblem and flying Bf 110C-4/Bs this unit flew strike missions almost constantly through the winter months of 1941-42. [Bundesarchiv]

66 Imp. Gal. Drop Tank

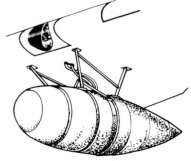

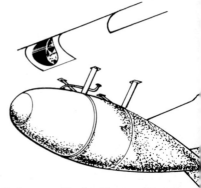

198 Imp. Gal. Drop Tank

[Above] While the severity of the Russian winter caught the Army unprepared, taking a severe toll of both men and equipment, the Luftwaffe was much better prepared, being issued winter clothing and equipment well in advance. [Bundesarchiv]

[Top] The Luftwaffe was able to maintain the serviceability of their machines at a very high percentage, curtailing operations during actual storms and bad weather. [Bundesarchiv]

was completed by 7 October, but the movement toward Moscow was slowed down by rain and the ensuing mud. By 13 November, however, cold had set in and the Panzer divisions were again on the move across the hardened ground toward Moscow, and by the 27th of November elements of the 3rd Panzergruppe reached the Volga canal just 19 miles from the center of Moscow. Bitterly cold weather and heavy snows had by now begun taking their toll of the Wehrmacht, which was totally unprepared for the severity of the Russian winter. On 5-6 December, just as the Germans decided to go over to the defensive, the Russians struck, launching a massive counter-attack hurling the Germans back from Moscow. Fighting continuous delaying actions, the Germans finally succeeded in establishing a new, but in places critically thin, defensive line.

When production of the Bf 110 had all but ceased during late 1941, the Zerstörergruppen also all but ceased to exist before the Bf 110 was put back in production during Feb. of 1942. The lack of Bf 110 production coupled with an increased demand for the twin engine fighter by the Nachtjagdverbände proved nearly disastrous for Zerstörer units at the end of 1941, when they all but disappeared from Luftwaffe strength reports. From a strength high of 444 machines on 10 August 1940, their numbers had fallen to 44 machines with only 28 being serviceable on 13 December 1941. The Luftwaffe's elite had now become a stepchild, a Cinderella whose fairy godmother would turn out to be the Allied daylight bomber armada during 1943.

During the course of 1942, with the Bf 110 again in production, Zerstörer strength was brought back up to a high of 300 machines, but monthly strength averaged only about 200 and serviceability was usually at less than

half. The Zerstörergruppen were as follows at the close of 1942:

I and II/ZG 1 (Formerly SKG 210)
I, II and III/ZG 26
13.(Z)/JG 5

A number of other units carrying the Zerstörer designation such as III/ZG 1 and ZG 2 were in fact equipped with Fw 190s or Me 210 fighter bombers. Starved for aircraft, the Zerstörergruppen fared poorly during 1942, playing its most important role in North Africa where ZG 26 had been the first Luftwaffe formation to arrive in the theater. When the British launched their massive assault at El Alamein at the end of October 1942, 8./ZG 26 was over 300 miles away at Derna while 7. and 9./ZG 76 were even further, being at Kastelli on Crete. Used mainly to protect convoys plying the Mediterranean, their first loss after the beginning of the El Alamein offensive was a machine that accidentally force landed in a mine field on 3 November, the crew being killed. With German ground forces falling back, III/ZG 26 was also called upon to carry out protective patrols above the retreat-choked roads.

On 8 November 1942, four days after Rommel had begun his retreat, Anglo-American forces began landing in French North Africa and the Luftwaffe began switching units from all points to the Mediterranean area to meet this new threat. III/ZG 26 was moved to Sicily where it was used almost exclusively to escort both sea and air transport and only occasionally seen over North Africa. The step-up of Allied daylight bombings during the summer of 1943 finally caused this crack Zerstörer unit to return to Germany.

Bf 110E

Even though production of the Bf 110 was being run down in anticipation of its replacement by the Me 210, two further versions, the Bf 110E and Bf 110F, were put into full production during the middle of 1941. The first of these two aircraft, the Bf 110E, began to come off the assembly line during early spring. Other than internal armor improvements and structural strengthening there was no external change from earlier models. The undercarriage was beefed up considerably, so increased bomb loads could be carried. The fighter - bomber could carry four ETC 50 racks under the outboard wings or two 66 Imp. gal. drop tanks in addition to the center line bomb rack.

Bf 110E-1 Zerstörer -	initially powered by the DB 601A engine but very quickly standardized on the DB 601N engine.
Bf 110E-1/U2	provided space for a third crew member.
Bf 110E-1 Jabo	had an extended tail for stowage of a dinghy.
Bf 110E-3 Reconnaissance -	This version had the forward firing MG-FF and ventral rack removed and a camera installed in the floor. Either a pair of 66 Imp. gal. or two 198 Imp. gal. drop tanks could be carried.

The increased offensive bomb load was especially welcomed on the Eastern Front where SKG 210 was constantly engaged in carrying out low level attacks on Soviet forces. [Bundesarchiv]

Additional Rear Firing MG17s on some Bf 110E-3s

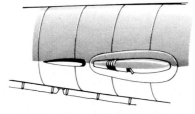

The four wing mounted ETC 50 bomb racks, standardized on the E series, could carry a 110 lb. bomb on each, thus raising the maximum bomb load to 2,645 lbs. [Bundesarchiv]

The hand hydraulic bomb loader made rearming the Zerstörer Jabos a quick and efficient task. Without this machine the armourers task would have been a back-breaking chore. [Bundesarchiv]

As on the Eastern Front, the increased bomb load was also a most welcome addition in the Western Desert where the surprise hit and run tactics were very effective. The Handley Page automatic slot can be seen in an extended position.

A number of Zerstörer operating in the desert areas of North Africa were quickly fitted with an external dust filter as seen on this Bf 110E of 7./ZG 26. [Bundesarchiv]

A Bf 110 of 8./ZG 26 escorts a flight of Ju 52s over the Western Desert. Because of the distances involved, much needed supplies were often times flown to front line troops. [Gene Stafford]

Bf 110F

Introduced shortly after the E series, the Bf 110F was powered by a pair of 1,350 h.p. DB 601F engines. The only external differences being an increase in the size of the engine nacelle mounted oil cooler and the installation of a 57mm bullet-resistant wind screen (retrospectively fitted to D and E models). Because the Bf 110 had been subject to a constant increase in equipment and a subsequent increase in operational weight with no increase in power, its performance had been steadily deteriorating. The increase in horsepower offered by the new DB 601F engine greatly improved the machine's performance allowing several variants to be built. 66 Imperial gal. drop tanks were standardized.

Bf 110F-1 fighter-bomber carrying an ETC 500 bomb rack on the centerline that could mount either a pair of 551 lb. SC 250 bombs, a pair of SC 500 bombs or an AB 500 container. The four wing ETC 50 racks could mount 110 lb. SC 50, SD 50 or an AB container.

Bf 110F-2 Zerstörer - standard fighter version that carried the same armament as earlier versions. Later a pair of WGr 21 rocket projections were added under each wing.

Bf 110F-3 Reconnaissance variant. As with the E-3 the twin MG-FF cannon were removed and a camera was mounted in the floor of the cockpit.

Engine Development

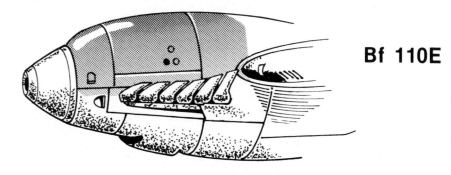

Bf 110E

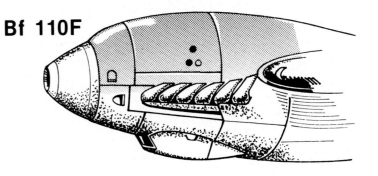

Bf 110F

Carrying the ZG 26 "Horst Wessel" insignia on its nose, and the wooden shoe symbol of II Gruppe, this Bf 110F-1 is seen on a mission over the Eastern Front during 1942, shortly before it was disbanded. [Bundesarchiv]

During the spring and summer of 1942, the new Bf 110F-2 Zerstörer began to arrive in the Western Desert. The increased performance of the F series was a welcome addition to the Luftwaffe, who were supporting Rommel's Drive to El Alamein. This Bf 110F-2 Zerstörer belonging to ZG 26 carries the tropical dust filters and two ETC 50 bomb racks under each wing. [Bundesarchiv]

Bf 110F-1 fighter-bombers of I/SKG 210 over the Eastern Front during the summer of 1942. [Ernie McDowell]

The Bf 110F-1 fighter-bomber carried a pair of ETC 500 racks beneath the fuselage capable of carrying two 551 lb. SC 500 general purpose, or SD 250 fragmentation bombs, two 1,102 lb. SC 500 bombs, or an AB 500 container of small incendiary or fragmentation bombs which discharged its contents by means of an airburst fuse. The bleakness of the terrain gives one an idea of the conditions often times encountered by the Luftwaffe in North Africa. [Bundesarchiv]

The Bf 110F-2 was used as a test bed for adapting the 21 cm Werfer-Granate [Wfr. Gr. 21] army nebelwerfer to aerial use. This installation would allow the intercepters to attack the bomber formations while remaining outside of the enemies defensive fire. Tested at Tarnewitz, the new weapon was an immediate success and it was decided to begin serial production for the forthcoming "G" series. [Hans Redemann]

Armored Windscreen

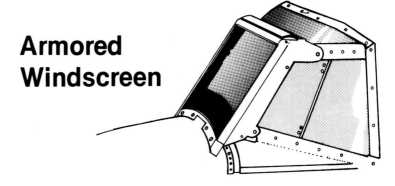

[Above Left] Looking more like a Bedouin, this ground crewman runs up the starboard engine on this F-3. A close look at the underside of the fuselage, just behind the wing root, will reveal the camera apperture opening on this tiger-striped machine. The 20mm MG FF openings are painted on in black. [Smithsonian Institution]

The 57mm bullet resistant windscreen, standardized on the F series, was retrofitted to all earlier models still in service. Simple Rüstsatze [field conversion sets] were supplied to the armorers which installed them easily. [Bundesarchiv]

Bf 110G

During 1941, it was anticipated that the Me 210 would replace the Bf 110 in first line units, consequently the Bf 110s production was ordered terminated with production ceasing at MIAG in October 1941 and GWF in December. Unfortunately the Me 210 proved to be an "abysmal failure", and deliveries of the Bf 110F were resumed in February 1942.

Steps had already been taken during the summer of 1941 to rejuvenate the basic design. Under the preproduction designation Bf 110G-0 the fuselage was aerodynamically cleaned up and was powered by a pair of DB 601F engines delivering 1,475 h.p. for take off and emergency landing and 1,355 h.p. at 18,700 ft. The initial production machine, the Bf 110G-1, had the MG-FF cannon replaced with a pair of MG 151 and the ETC bomb racks removed. The G-1 was not built, instead the Bf 110G-2, which, through the application of various Rüstsätze (Field Conversion Sets) could be used as either a Zerstörer or fighter bomber. These Rüstsätze made the G series the most versatile of the Bf 110s produced. The first Bf 110G-2 entered service in May of 1942.

Bf 110G-1 not built

Bf 110G-2 adopted the revised and enlarged vertical tail surfaces of the F-4 night fighter. Forward firing armament consisted of the four 7.9 MG 17s and a pair of 20mm MG 151 cannon. The ETC 500 bomb racks were standard but could be replaced with a weapon tray containing a pair of MG 151s. The two 66 Imp. gal. drop tanks were made interchangeable with four ETC 50 bomb racks.

Bf 110G-3 long range reconnaissance fighter carried a single Rd 50/30 and Rb 70/30 camera. As with earlier models the G-3s nose mounted armament was restricted to the four MG 17s although some machines replaced the MG 17s with a pair of Mk 108s (Rüstsatz 3).

Engine Development

Bf 110F

Engine

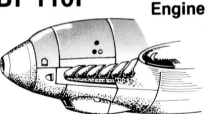

Bf 110G

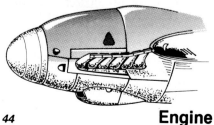

Engine

Tail

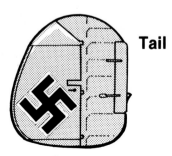

Tail

Early Bf 110G-2s of Stab I/SKG 210 over Russia during July 1942. Note the retention of the early vertical tail surfaces and the single rear firing MG 15. It is possible that these are pre-production G-0s. [Bundesarchiv]

The Bf 110G-2 began leaving assembly lines during May 1942 and could be utilized as either a Zerstörer or heavy fighter bomber through the application of various Rüstsätze. [Bundesarchiv]

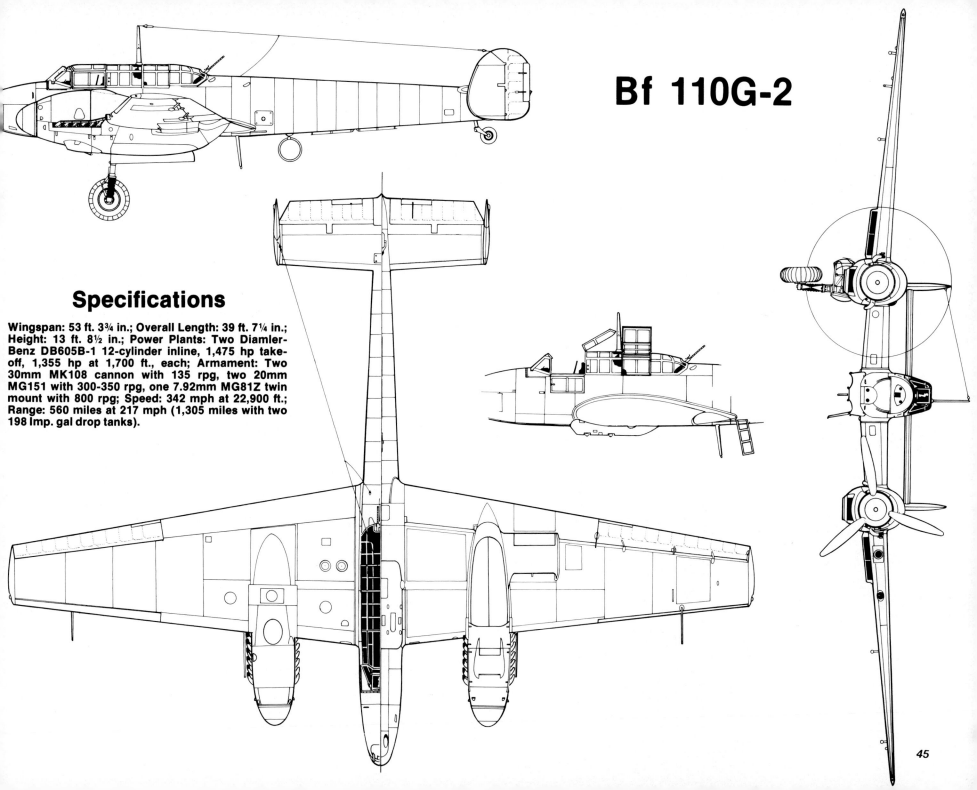

Bf 110G-2

Specifications

Wingspan: 53 ft. 3¾ in.; Overall Length: 39 ft. 7¼ in.; Height: 13 ft. 8½ in.; Power Plants: Two Diamler-Benz DB605B-1 12-cylinder inline, 1,475 hp take-off, 1,355 hp at 1,700 ft., each; Armament: Two 30mm MK108 cannon with 135 rpg, two 20mm MG151 with 300-350 rpg, one 7.92mm MG81Z twin mount with 800 rpg; Speed: 342 mph at 22,900 ft.; Range: 560 miles at 217 mph (1,305 miles with two 198 Imp. gal drop tanks).

Flying under the most adverse winter conditions 7.[Z]/JG 5 learned to keep their aircraft serviceable despite the bitter cold. Of note are the presence of ETC 50 bomb racks at the same time the machine is carrying 66 Imp. gal. auxiliary fuel tanks. [Bundesarchiv]

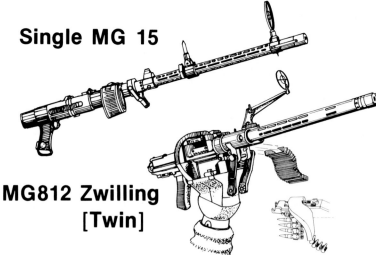

Single MG 15

MG812 Zwilling [Twin]

[Above Left] One of the few units still operating in the day Zerstörer role during the winter 1942-43 were the Zerstörer staffeln of JG 5. The increased performance of the "G" series had long been needed by this unit. [Bundesarchiv]

Oberleutnant Felix Brandis, Staffelkapitän of 10.[Z]/JG 5 on the right, and his radioman, Feldwebel Baus, are photographed beside the tail of their Bf 110 during the second winter of the war on the Eastern Front. Brandis had at least 18 victories. [Bundesarchiv]

The R1 Rüstsatz comprised a 37 mm. Bk 3.7 [Flak 18] cannon attached to the underside of the fuselage inside a light wood and fabric fairing. With a muzzle velocity of 3,840 ft./sec. it could usually disable a B-17 with one hit. Unfortunately the weapon made the Bf 110 unwieldly and even less maneuverable. [Hans Redemann]

Having been standard equipment since the Bf 110V-3 in 1936, the quartette of 7.9mm MG 17 machine guns were for the first time, replaced with Rüstsatz 3, comprising a pair of 30mm Mk 108 cannon. [Gene Stafford]

Rüstsätze

R1 37mm. Bk 3.7 [Flak 18] cannon [Required the removal of the ventral MG 151s]

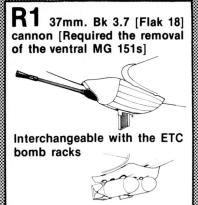

Interchangeable with the ETC bomb racks

R2 GM1 Powerboost-nitrous oxide injection system

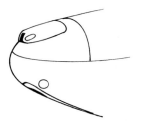

Weight of system required the removal of the nose armament

R4 both Rüstsätze 1 & 3

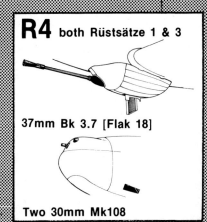

37mm Bk 3.7 [Flak 18]

Two 30mm Mk108

R3 Two 30mm Mk 108 replaced the four 7.9mm MG 17 machine guns

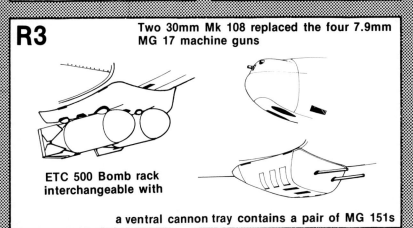

ETC 500 Bomb rack interchangeable with

a ventral cannon tray contains a pair of MG 151s

R5 Incorporating 1, 2, 3 GM1 nitrous oxide injection system and 37mm BK 3.7 [Flak 18] or

ETC 500 Bomb rack or

a twin MG 151 ventral tray

R6 Incorporating 2 and 3 GM1 nitrous oxide injection system

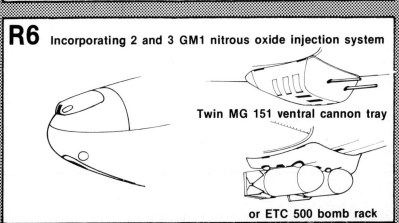

Twin MG 151 ventral cannon tray

or ETC 500 bomb rack

R7 119 Imperial gal. fuel tank in Radio operator's compartment

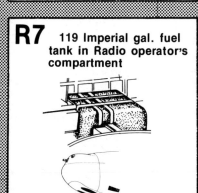

and R3 30mm Mk 108

DEFENSE OF THE REICH

Germany itself was now becoming the new crisis point of the Air War, as huge formations of Allied bombers began ravaging her war industries. By Autumn 1943, the Zerstörergruppen had been resurrected as part of the "Defense of the Reich" including I. and II/ZG 1, III/ZG 26 (I/ZG 1 became I/ZG 26 and a second gruppe was added shortly to bring ZG 26 up to full three gruppen strength). In October ZG 76 with I. and II Gruppe under Oberst Theodor Rossiwall were formed with a III Gruppe being added in November. By 10 November twin engine fighter strength had been brought up to 340 machines but many of the pilots were still only partially trained, even by current Luftwaffe standards. But since American bombers were still operating without fighter cover over much of Germany, losses were kept to a minimum and successes were high.

Fortunately for the Allies, weather had in the main kept the massed Zerstörer and American heavies apart until 11 January 1944 when 650 heavies were sent deep into Germany to attack the aircraft factories in the Braunschweig (Brunswick) area. The massed Bf 110s of the Zerstörergruppen poured their 240 mm rockets into the tightly packed groups, breaking up the bombers protective formations, then join the Bf 109s in attacking individual aircraft. 41 bombers failed to return. On 16 March, forty-three Bf 110s of ZG 76 caught the heavies without fighter protection and knocked down 18 B-17s. After their third pass, however, the bomber's escort arrived and dived to the attack. During the ensuing air battle 26 (60%) of the Zerstörer were shot down. After such heavy losses, ZG 76 disbanded its III gruppe and reequipment of the Zerstörergruppen with Me 410s was made top priority. By June 1944, only II/ZG 1 was still operational on the Bf 110. Forced further and further eastward by American fighter escorts one of the last daylight Zerstörer operations participated in by Bf 110s was fought over Budapest where II/ZG 1 (Bf 110s), in concert with I/ZG 76 (Me 410s) and II/JG 77 (Bf 109s), claimed some 45 Allied aircraft. Shortly after this II/ZG 1 traded its Bf 110s for Bf 109Gs becoming II/JG 76 in the process. Thus ended the checkered career of one of the most enigmatic fighters of World War II.

This Bf 110G-2 heavy fighter bomber in Southern Russia coded Q1 + VB catches fire when the ground personnel tries to start the port DB 605 engine. The skeletal insignia on the nose is of particular interest but is as yet unidentified. [Bundesarchiv]

In 1942, II/SKG 210 was renamed II/ZG 1 and shortly sent to Italy. This unit had now come full circle. Originally it had been 1. Staffel ZG 1 and when 2. and 3. Staffel were transferred to the night fighters, it remained behind becoming the nucleus of E.Gr. 210. In 1941, the unit was redesignated II/SKG 210 and participated in the invasion of Russia. Always retaining its Wespen [wasp] insignia the unit now found itself again in the Zerstörer role under the designation II/ZG 1 although its doubtful that any of the original pilots survived until this took place. [Bundesarchiv]

The summer of 1943 found II/ZG 1 operating their Bf 110G-2s as a Zerstörer unit over the Italian mainland. [Bundesarchiv]

When the Wfr. Gr. 21 rocket launching tubes were carried on the Bf 110G-2/R3, the twin Mk 108 cannon were removed but in order to not lose fire power the interchangeable ETC 500 bomb carriers were replaced by the twin MG 151 cannon tray. [Bundesarchiv]

Once in the air, the rocket equipped machines would climb to just above the bomber formation. The rockets could be fired from a range of just over 6,000 feet and still be grouped 50 percent in a circle of 97 feet, with the remainder in a circle of 200 feet. Operationally, the fuses were usually set to be fired at from 1800 to 3600 feet. Weighing 248 pounds with a ninety lb. warhead this weapon was initially very effective in breaking up the closely packed B-17 formations. When the bomber formations broke up, the Zerstörer and single engine fighters could then attack the bombers singly. [Bundesarchiv]

As the 8th Air Forces daylight bombing offensive increased during the summer of 1943, the Luftwaffe breathed new life into the Zerstörer gruppen. I and II/ZG 1 and III/ZG 26 were transferred to the defense of the Reich. I/ZG 1 became I/ZG 26 and II/ZG 26 was reformed bringing "Horst Wessel" to full strength. During October ZG76 was reestablished. [Bundesarchiv]

On 16 March 1944, forty-three Bf 110Gs from ZG 76 intercepted an American bomber force on its way to Augsburg. Initially the twin engine Zerstörer were able to press home their attack, but before they could make a third pass, P-51 Mustangs of the 354th Fighter Squadron swept in. During the next few minutes the Mustangs downed 26 Bf 110s. Within weeks III/ZG 76 was disbanded. [Bundesarchiv]